HOW TO
LEAD
Small
Groups

NEAL F. McBRIDE

NAVPRESS ®
A MINISTRY OF THE NAVIGATORS
P.O. BOX 35001, COLORADO SPRINGS, COLORADO 80935

OUR GUARANTEE TO YOU

We believe so strongly in the message of our books that we are making this quality guarantee to you. If for any reason you are disappointed with the content of this book, return the title page to us with your name and address and we will refund to you the list price of the book. To help us serve you better, please briefly describe why you were disappointed. Mail your refund request to: NavPress, P.O. Box 35002, Colorado Springs, CO 80935.

The Navigators is an international Christian organization. Our mission is to reach, disciple, and equip people to know Christ and to make Him known through successive generations. We envision multitudes of diverse people in the United States and every other nation who have a passionate love for Christ, live a lifestyle of sharing Christ's love, and multiply spiritual laborers among those without Christ.

NavPress is the publishing ministry of The Navigators. NavPress publications help believers learn biblical truth and apply what they learn to their lives and ministries. Our mission is to stimulate spiritual formation among our readers.

Unless otherwise noted, Scripture quotations in this publication are from the *New American Standard Bible* (NASB).© The Lockman Foundation 1960, 1962, 1968, 1971, 1972, 1973, 1975, 1977. Another version used is the *Holy Bible New International Version* (NIV). Copyright © 1973, 1978, 1984, International Bible Society. Used by permission of Zondervan Bible Publishers.

Printed in the United States of America

15 16 17 18 19/04 03 02 01

FOR A FREE CATALOG OF
NAVPRESS BOOKS & BIBLE STUDIES,
CALL 1-800-366-7788 (USA)
or 1-416-499-4615 (CANADA)

Contents

To
Reva, Kyle, and Katie—
my wife and children,
my most important small group

Author

Dr. Neal McBride has served as president of Grace University and as Dean of Graduate and Continuing Studies at Bethel College in St. Paul, Minnesota. He is now executive director of operations for The National Network of Estate Planning Attorneys, a service organization for attorneys. He is a recognized small-group expert and the author of several books, including *How to Lead Small Groups, How to Have Great Small-Groups, How to Have Great Small-Group Meetings,* and *How to Build a Small-Groups Ministry.*

Introduction

Have you ever wished you could just look into Jesus' eyes and see His concern when you told Him about something that hurts? Have you ever wished you could feel His strong arms give you a comforting hug? Have you ever wanted to see His eyes shine when you trusted Him and He showed Himself faithful? How much easier depending on Jesus and communing with Him would be if only He were here where we could see Him! That's exactly why He gave us each other: to be His serving hands, empathizing heart, listening ears, and encouraging words. Caringroup is Jesus' body! The people in my group are what Jesus, who is in Heaven, can't be to me.

Being involved in a small group is an opportunity for in-depth fellowship and friendships. It is a place to bear burdens and celebrate victories. It's a place to give and receive inspiration, to live up to God's best. A small group experience is not all serious. Warmth and acceptance is the best atmosphere for fun and relaxation, spontaneous get-togethers, and building life-long friendships. For me, caringroup has meant the difference between church attendance and being a part of our church family.

Marie Stingle
Portland, Oregon
August 1989

FROM THE AUTHOR

Wouldn't it be terrific if the members of your group felt the same way Marie does! I hope that you're reading this book because you want to learn how to be an effective group leader. Whether you're a new leader with no background in small groups, an old hand with vast experience, or somewhere in between, I'm positive that this short volume will serve you well.

Over the years I've found that the topic of small group leadership can be divided into two distinct, but related, topics. First, and the focus of this book, is the issue of one person leading one group. In this instance the focus is on one individual group. I refer to this one-to-one group approach simply as "small group leadership." The second topic, one that is much larger in scope, deals with organizing and administering many groups, or a whole groups' ministry. This type of leadership demands leading other small group leaders. A phrase such as "small group management" seems appropriate. This latter topic is only alluded to in this handbook.

Since the focus is on leading your individual group, this book is written to achieve three goals:

 ◆ To establish a clear biblical basis for small groups;
 ◆ To provide a basic introduction to the dynamics of leading a small group; and
 ◆ To present a sampling of topics, methods, tasks, and skills associated with being an effective group leader.

Given these three goals, each of the seven chapters attempts to accomplish a specific objective. By the time you finish reading these chapters, you should be able to do the following:

 Chapter 1—Defend the biblical basis for small groups.
 Chapter 2—Outline the requirements and tasks of group
     leadership.
 Chapter 3—Describe the phases of your group's development.
 Chapter 4—Identify the specific characteristics of your group.
 Chapter 5—Perform various tasks and functions associated
     with group leadership.

Chapter 6—Develop a strategy for coping with conflict and problems your group may encounter.

Chapter 7—Evaluate the progress and outcomes of your group.

Read, enjoy, and grow in your knowledge and appreciation for a ministry of great significance . . . small group leader!

CHAPTER ONE

The Biblical Foundations for Small Groups

T he most important thing you need to know as a small group leader is the biblical foundation for your ministry. We'll look at the biblical roots and requirements, then briefly consider additional facts that support the need for groups. Pay close attention so that you don't miss anything, because this information will help you grasp the significance of your role as a small group leader.

The small group ministry is founded on a rock-hard biblical base. This firm foundation guards against the storms of change brought about by the many programmatic fads that blow through our churches. Although initially these fads seem exciting and potentially beneficial, they quickly subside because they lack a clear biblical basis. Small groups are not one of these fanciful fads. In fact, of all the potential ministry formats available to the local church, *small groups have the greatest biblical support!* Consequently, it is important for you as a small group leader to understand and appreciate the rich biblical heritage that precedes you.

OLD TESTAMENT ROOTS

The basis of today's small group ministries can be traced back to the Old Testament. The small group begins with the very nature of God. Genesis 1:1 launches the biblical record with a simple yet profound statement that God (*Elohim*) is the Creator of all that exists. The word *Elohim* is plural, designating or incorporating more than one person.

Although interpreted as singular throughout the Old Testament, the word expresses the unity of three persons in the one God—the Father, the Son, and the Holy Spirit. These three share jointly in the same nature and majesty of God—a unique relationship beyond our mere human comprehension. Yet, the Trinity pictures for us the pivotal concept of relationships within a group. Our own need for and use of groups is a logical extension of the fact that God exists within the divine form of a small group. Of course, the term *small group* is not used in Scripture, but neither is the word *Trinity.*

The concept of groups is pictured further in the Old Testament record of God's chosen people, the Israelites. The notion and practice of groups was tightly woven into the fabric of their individual and corporate identities. From the entire nation down to the smallest family unit, a large and small group mentality permeated the Jewish existence.

Nation—The Israelites were a chosen people; God set them apart from all other peoples on the face of the earth (Deuteronomy 7:6). They were a select and unique group within human creation. They were chosen not because they were large in number, but because they were few in number and God loved them (Deuteronomy 7:7-8). They formed a great family called "the house of Israel" (Exodus 40:38). This family identity served as the model around which the nation was internally organized.

Tribe—The house of Israel, by virtue of its descent from the twelve sons of Jacob, was divided into twelve subgroups or tribes (Genesis 49). Tribes provided the leaders with a method to administer and guide the people. These tribal subgroupings were established clearly by the time the land of Canaan was divided among the Israelites according to their tribes and families (Joshua 13–22).

Family or clan—Tribes were broken down further into groups of relatives known as clans or families. By the last year of the Israelites' wilderness journey, fifty-seven families existed among the twelve tribes. The families were formed from Jacob's grandchildren and by the grandchildren and great-grandchildren of the twelve heads of the tribes. Numbers 26:21-49 profiles the families with their associated tribes.

Household—This literally means "house." The various clans were divided down into family subgroups or relatives living in the same dwelling, including servants and dependents. This is the idea when Scripture speaks of "the household of Joseph" (Genesis 50:8) or "Pharaoh and all his household" (Deuteronomy 6:22). Households typically incorporated several generations of relatives and servants.

Fathers or men—A specific man, including his wife and children, was the smallest group within the Jewish identity. The phrases "son of" and "daughter of" were common social identifiers, linking the person to his or her father. A single family unit could exist as part of a larger household or as a separate entity. Individual family units were the heart of Jewish society—the primary small groups.

Every Jew could (and many still can) rehearse his or her identity based on nation, tribe, family, household, and father. These identity groupings were important political, social, and spiritual designations.

JESUS AS A SMALL GROUP LEADER

Jesus Christ is pictured as the greatest small group leader in history. He is our model. Ephesians 5:1-2 (NIV) admonishes us, "Be imitators of God . . . and live a life of love." Clearly, the primary idea of the Apostle Paul is becoming Christlike in our character. However, to focus solely on character formation is to catch only half of the author's intent. We also must seek to imitate Christ's walk—His behavior or actions that were marked by love.

How does a person become Christlike? How does one learn to walk in love? In what contexts does a Christian experience Christlikeness and become Christlike? Answers to these questions are not simple. Nevertheless, on close examination of the New Testament's record of the life and ministry of Jesus, it becomes clear that one key method is *small groups.*

For me, Jesus' involvement in a small group is the most convincing rationale for why local churches need to seriously consider including groups as an integral part of their congregational lives. While it may not be wise or even appropriate for believers to mimic Jesus' every *act* (i.e., healing a blind man by spitting on his eyes [Mark 8:23]), it is logical to replicate those behavioral patterns that constituted His methods for ministry. Therefore, it makes tremendous sense to explore Jesus' use of small groups.

As a small group leader, you are involved in a form of leadership in which our Lord and Savior also participated. You are walking in His footsteps. So, increasing your knowledge and understanding of small group leadership is essential. The heart of what you need to know about Jesus as a small group leader can be summarized in seven key statements.

First, Jesus began His earthly ministry by *establishing* His "small group," the disciples. One of Jesus' first acts in beginning His public ministry was to form His small group (Matthew 4:18-22, Luke 6:13-16). Matthew 10:2-4 lists the names of the group members, the twelve men Jesus chose. The Son of God certainly didn't need the companionship or assistance of the disciples. Yet, from the very beginning, He elected to establish and minister within a framework of interpersonal relationships. Among all the disciples who sought to follow Jesus, the Twelve were members of Jesus' designated inner group. It was a human application or representation of the divine relationship Jesus possesses as a member of the Trinity.

Second, Jesus was actively involved in *both* large and small group ministry contexts. Large group and small group ministries were not pitted against one another. Nor was it the case of one or the other exclusively. He proclaimed His Kingdom to large crowds and was well received (Mark 12:37). Likewise, He met with small groups in homes (Matthew 26:6) and spent considerable time with His special group, the Twelve.

Third, we see that Jesus' ministry to large groups was preceded by and proceeded out of His small group context. Which came first, the chicken (large group) or the egg (small group)? In the case of Jesus' public ministry, His small group emphasis preceded His large group involvement. Furthermore, it was the small group that provided the platform for Jesus' ministry to large groups of people. It was common for Jesus to have the twelve disciples with Him as He proclaimed the good news to the multitudes. Yet, He often withdrew to the familiarity and support of His select small group (Mark 3:7).

Fourth, Jesus spent the majority of His time with His small group. If it were possible to add up the actual amount of time Jesus spent with the disciples, likely the results would show that this group consumed the majority of His time. They were together constantly; they traveled together, shared meals, experienced mutual hardship, and literally lived together. As Jesus' crucifixion drew closer, He spent more and more time with His small group, but less and less time with the multitudes that sought Him out.

The fifth key statement about Jesus as a small group leader is that relationships, not organizations, were central in His method. Jesus gave little, if any, time and attention to building an earthly organization. The Kingdom He sought to proclaim was not a material organization, but rather a heavenly realm (Luke 17:20-21). His message, the gospel, was of greater concern to Him than establishing and running a human institution. Christ could have easily remained aloof from any relationships that entangled Him in human needs and suffering. Yet, as a practical demonstration of the gospel, He chose to spend His time with people, caring, healing, listening, forgiving, encouraging, teaching, and preaching. Because of His emphasis on people, not programs, the only organization that merited Jesus' continuing time and attention was His small group. (And it never was classified as an organization or program.)

Sixth, we see that Jesus used the small group context to teach and model spiritual knowledge, attitudes, and behavior. Having formed His group, Jesus taught and modeled spiritual truth by simply drawing them close to Himself. It was not a formal or academic experience. The small group members simply participated with Christ in whatever He did. They saw and experienced the attitudes and actions He was admonishing others to adopt. Their association preceded Jesus' explanations. It was through this intimacy that the Twelve were "granted to know the mysteries of the kingdom of God" (Luke 8:10). The small group was their living-learning laboratory.

Finally, the small group was Jesus' method for leadership training. He devoted Himself primarily to the task of developing a select group of men, the Apostles. His goal was to equip this small group of disciples to carry on the work of the gospel after He returned to the Father. Success was to be measured in terms of their future ministries, not in present achievements. Jesus selected common men—unlearned and ignorant by worldly standards (Acts 4:13)—who were ready to follow Him and were teachable. In turn, He poured His life into these men and thrust the future of His whole ministry on them. (See John 17.) They received God's Word (verse 14) and Jesus' protection (verse 12). Thanking the Father for "the men whom Thou gavest Me out of the world" (verse 6), Jesus further asked for their sanctification "in the truth" (verse 17). It would be "through their word" that many would come to believe (verse 20).

THE EARLY CHURCH AS AN EXAMPLE

From the very beginning, small groups were integral to the church's development and success. This fact is not surprising given the background of the people involved, their social context, and the nature of the church.

A majority of the first Christians were Jews. Only later did the Apostle Paul take the good news to the Gentiles (Acts 9:15). As a result, the early church reflected a strong Jewish, Old Testament flavor, including its emphasis on groups. The individual family unit was the center of Jewish religious and social instruction, and this practice was carried through into the New Testament era. It is no wonder that small groups became a natural element of the early church.

The home played an essential and critical role in Jewish society. It was the context for many family and community activities. The house church became a natural expression of this emphasis. In fact, apart from those referred to in a general geographic location, the only congregations mentioned in the epistles were those in specific homes. The churches that met in the homes of Priscilla and Aquila (Romans 16:3-5) and Philemon (verse 2) are examples.

One of Paul's major metaphors for describing the church was a family household. He encouraged the Galatians to "do good to all men, and especially to those who are of the household of the faith" (Galatians 6:10). He offered encouragement to the believers in Ephesus by reminding them that they were members "of God's household" (Ephesians 2:19). He used this same word picture in writing to his friend Timothy (1 Timothy 3:15).

The Apostle Peter also used the household metaphor. He called the church "the household of God" (1 Peter 4:17), and he further expanded the idea as "a spiritual house" (1 Peter 2:5). Both Peter and Paul viewed the church as a spiritual family and the Body of Christ (another favorite metaphor). The terms *house* and *household* capitalized on this image and its inherent relationships.

Acts 2:42-47 gives us a glimpse of how the Jerusalem household of God (church) functioned. It was an exciting time. We are given an outline of their activities: "They were continually devoting themselves to the apostles' teaching and to fellowship, to the breaking of bread and to prayer" (verse 42). A balance existed among instruction, fellowship, common activities (meals), and spiritual responsibilities (prayer). The atmosphere was charged. A sense of awe, unity, and praise prevailed. People looked out for one another. They sold their property and possessions, sharing the proceeds with those in need. This dynamic situation brought the approval of all people. Spiritual and numerical growth were evident. God was at work in their midst.

Individual homes contributed to the success: "Day by day continuing with one mind in the temple, and breaking bread *from house to house,* they were taking their meals together with gladness and sincerity of heart" (Acts 2:46, emphasis added). "Every day, in the temple and from house to house, they kept right on teaching and preaching Jesus as the Christ" (5:42). Later we see Paul active in teaching and evangelizing "from house to house" (20:20). Meetings in houses provided the backbone of the church structure. But as central as they were, homes were not the only context in which the Jerusalem church functioned.

Large mass meetings were also a part of the accepted routine. The believers met in the temple as well as in homes. It was natural for them to gravitate to the settings with which they were most familiar. The temple and synagogues were such settings. While the dynamics of the church community were served by these mass meetings, frequently the focus was on nonbelievers with an evangelistic emphasis (Acts 3:11-26, 6:9-10, 8:4-8, 17:1-4).

Large public meetings became more difficult as time passed. The church began to encounter increasing persecution. Followers of Jesus Christ found they were unwelcome in the temple, synagogues, and public forums. Small home meetings, therefore, took on an even greater significance. Nevertheless, it would be a mistake to conclude that house churches were exclusively a result of persecution. Before or during and with or without persecution, active participation in a house church was not considered an option—*it was the norm!*

The house church remained the most pervasive form of church structure up until the time of Constantine about 274-337 AD—reputedly the first Christian emperor of Rome. From that time on church buildings (basilicas, cathedrals, chapels) began to displace the house church. By around 1250 AD, the Gothic cathedral had reached its pinnacle of popularity. As a result, the erroneous theological perception that the *church was a building, not a body of people* had become commonplace. Since then history has given us a variety of renewal movements that have challenged this perception. Some people, including myself, would argue that another such movement is beginning to catch fire today. The contemporary resurgence of small groups as a tool for renewal and growth is an attempt to enable the church to realize its full potential. However, the "building mentality" is persistent and continues to present us with a formidable uphill battle.

THE NEW TESTAMENT MANDATE

Much of the New Testament, if not the majority, deals with the attitudes and actions God would have characterize the members of His household, the community of believers. Consider some of the "one another" verses:

> "Be devoted . . . [and] give preference to one another."
>   (Romans 12:10)
> "Accept one another." (Romans 15:7)
> "Care for one another." (1 Corinthians 12:25)
> "Bear one another's burdens." (Galatians 6:2)
> "Forgiving each other." (Ephesians 4:32)
> "Encourage . . . and build up one another." (1 Thessalonians
>   5:11)
> "Stimulate one another to love and good deeds." (Hebrews
>   10:24)
> "Confess your sins to . . . and pray for one another." (James
>   5:16)
> "Serving one another." (1 Peter 4:10)
> "Love one another." (1 John 4:11)

This list provides only a brief taste of the standards that should govern the household of God. Even so, the obvious question must be asked: What is the best setting or ideal method to pursue these biblical attitudes and actions? Certainly more than one answer is possible, but based on the biblical evidence, a logical answer is *small groups meeting in homes.* This ideal context stresses relationships in an informal setting, which in turn helps us understand and implement the New Testament mandate. This fact was true for the early church, and it is still true for us today.

Hebrews 10:24-25 provides us with further insight. Here we are instructed to not forsake (forget or abandon) our assembling together. Our usual contemporary response to this mandate is to assume we are being urged to attend "church"—a Sunday morning service held in a church building. Certainly this application is legitimate, but it's not inherent in the author's intent. Specifically, we are told "to stimulate one another to love and good deeds" and to "encourage one another." Such activities are possible in a large group service, but not probable. On the other hand, the small group's relational dynamic provides the ideal setting.

The words of Jesus found in Matthew 18:20 are very important: "For where two or three have gathered together in My name, there I am in their midst." Two or three *hundred* people aren't required. The vertical relationship each Christian enjoys with Jesus is facilitated and expanded by the horizontal relationships among the required two or three. Thus, I suggest, two Christians are the bare minimum to constitute a Christian community. This leads to the conclusion that "church" is not limited to the customary large meetings, but also can be a legitimate function of small groups.

Our mandate is not limited to an internal focus, a secret society for believers only. Jesus opens membership in the household of God to everyone when He commands us to "make disciples of all the nations" (Matthew 28:19). To achieve this dimension of the mandate, here again small groups can play a significant role. Paul understood this. His efforts in mass evangelism and instruction were augmented by personal evangelism and teaching in the various private homes (Acts 19:8-10, 20:20-21). The conversion of Cornelius and his whole household is an example (Acts 16:32-34).

Evangelism—and the larger issue of discipleship—is greatly enhanced in the relational context of small groups. Groups provide a people-to-people setting rather than a program-to-people agenda. This more natural, interpersonal context readily lends itself to sharing the gospel. This was shown by a 1988 study on religion in the United States done by the Princeton Religion Research Center under the direction of George Gallup, Jr., which cited small groups as "the outreach tool of the '90s."

In summary, the biblical support for small groups is overwhelming. Beginning in the Old Testament and continuing through the New Testament, small groups are pictured as an integral part of believers' lives. But most significantly, we know that the Lord Jesus ministered in the context of a small group. Consequently, I am willing to assert that small groups are a *necessity* in the local church, not merely a programmatic option. Your small group is in part a recognition of this necessity. Your leadership in this ministry format has deep biblical roots and is ideal for accomplishing the biblical mandate. Congratulations!

THE HOLY SPIRIT AS A GROUP MEMBER

An important foundation undergirding your role as a small group leader is the place of the Holy Spirit within the group. Simply put, He is the unseen but present group member and leader. You serve as His co-leader, the human instrument of His guidance and direction. Your primary role is to facilitate the Holy Spirit's ministry in the members' lives through planning and guiding the group activities. Please weld this reality into your thinking and actions, because it is vital to your success as a leader and to the group's success.

In condensed form, here are seven ministries the Holy Spirit performs in your group.

He indwells (Romans 8:9-11). The Scriptures are clear that the Holy Spirit dwells in every person who has accepted Jesus Christ as Savior. The Holy Spirit is present whenever Christians gather together. This means that He is present at every group meeting. We must acknowledge this fact and act accordingly.

He guides (John 16:13). As with individual believers, the Holy Spirit also provides guidance within small groups. Whether the issue is making scheduling decisions, selecting a format, responding to the Word, dealing with an obstinate member, rejoicing over one person's personal success, or anything else, we must remain sensitive to His guidance and direction. This process isn't always easy. Yet every effort must be exerted to practice following His leadership and discerning the will of God.

He teaches (John 14:26). The Holy Spirit is our teacher. Through His illumination of the biblical text, we can come to know and understand spiritual truth. In teaching us He may use a fellow group member to explain or illustrate from that person's life the spiritual truth being considered.

He convicts (John 16:8). When we are confronted with the demands of Scripture, it is the Holy Spirit who bears witness with our spirits and convicts us of our wrong attitudes and actions. The Spirit may convict all of the group members simultaneously. It is possible that an entire group needs to turn away from some attitude and/or action that is displeasing to God.

He intercedes (Romans 8:26). The Holy Spirit intercedes with God the Father on our behalf. Our corporate prayers reinforce individual prayers. In our spiritual weakness, the Spirit helps us in pleading our case before God. Individually and corporately, we have One who indwells us, knows our deepest needs, and makes intercession within us while Jesus Christ makes intercession for us at the right hand of God.

He enables (1 Corinthians 12:11). Spiritual gifts are God-given abilities to serve the Body of Christ wherever and however He may direct. The Holy Spirit is the source of our spiritual gifts. Through His gifting us we have the ability to serve one another, specifically our fellow group members.

He unifies (Ephesians 4:3). As God's children we are one people. The same Spirit makes us one and does all the things previously mentioned. Our practical unity as a group is possible on the basis of our spiritual unity through the Holy Spirit.

DEFINING SMALL GROUP

How would you define *small group* in the context of the local church? This is an important question. Having a definition is critical, because it identifies the characteristics of the activity you have agreed to lead. So, allow me to define what I mean when I use the words *small group*. Other definitions are possible, but here is a generic definition:

A small group within the church is a voluntary, intentional gathering of three to twelve people regularly meeting together with the shared goal of mutual Christian edification and fellowship.

A lot is packed into this definition. So, let's examine it closely by taking it apart phrase by phrase.

Within the church—The focus of our definition, and this book, is on groups within the context and ministry of the church, the Body of Christ (Romans 12:5). This distinction is important because small groups are used in many other contexts: education, business, military, government, and so on. This make sense, because small groups are an excellent method to facilitate human interaction and accomplishment. However, groups within the church, unlike most other groups, have a defined spiritual dimension and purpose to their existence. As such, they exist and operate under the direction of the Holy Spirit, utilizing biblical values and standards.

Voluntary—People cannot and should not be forced to join a small group. Potential group members must choose to participate. It can be argued that group membership is a spiritual obligation or duty, but this arm twisting technique doesn't produce long-term participation. People need to know, understand, see, and experience the value of being in a group. Salvation cannot be forced on people; likewise, group attendance must not be forced.

Intentional gathering—Small groups are premeditated, planned gatherings of people. They aren't random happenings left to chance. Clear purpose and design characterize the types of groups included in our definition. They systematically bring people together for deliberate reasons.

Three to twelve people—Group size is very important. When group membership expands beyond twelve people, it becomes increasingly difficult to maintain effective interpersonal relationships and accomplish the group's goals. This doesn't mean groups larger than twelve people won't work, but the likelihood of their success is reduced in proportion to their increased size. Jesus' group consisted of only twelve people besides Himself. If a group of this size was adequate for Jesus, who was God, we would do well to follow His example. (The topic of group size will come up again.)

Regularly meeting together—Groups can exist only on paper and never meet. Such groups fall outside our definition. We are concerned with groups that gather together on a consistent and frequent basis. Meetings are scheduled for a specific length of time, on an exact day, at a definite time and place. My preference is one-and-a-half hours, on a week night, 7:00 to 8:30 p.m., in my or another group member's home. We will explore other options later.

With the shared goal—The purpose of the group is not a secret for the leader to know and everyone else to find out. Members participating in groups that fit within the ideal definition understand, accept, and actively promote common goals. The general purpose for the existence of the group is openly acknowledged and approved by the group leader and members alike. While many specific goals and objectives may guide the existence of a group, the following two general goals are of mutual pursuit.

Mutual—The familiar adage "one for all and all for one" captures this aspect of the definition. Every member of the group actively must accept the responsibility for the group's success. There can be no idle observers, only active participants. Members must view their involvement as a blend of both giving to and receiving from the group. The leader *and* the members are accountable for group relationships, processes, tasks, and goals. This common responsibility is focused on two broad areas, discussed next.

Christian edification—The Greek words for *edify* (*oikodomeo*) and *edification* (*oikodome*) literally mean to "build" or "building up." Add the word *Christian* and the meaning focuses on the idea of strengthening or reinforcing the spiritual lives of believers. Therefore, regardless of the group's specific purpose or activities—evangelism, Bible study, prayer, sharing, worship—everything should be aimed at building people up to know, love, and serve Christ more and more. The Apostle Paul established this standard. In referring to the activities that ensued when the Corinthian church was assembled together, he instructed, "Let all things be done for edification" (1 Corinthians 14:26).

Fellowship—Our definition recognizes fellowship (*koinonia*) as the dynamic that builds and holds a small group together. I'm referring to more than merely coffee and donuts. Biblical fellowship carries the idea of communion with one another as an expression of our relationship with Jesus Christ (1 Corinthians 1:9). Fellowship was one of the key characteristics of the first church (Acts 2:42). In 1 John 1:7, we are told that if we "walk in the light" we have fellowship with one another. Small groups provide the context for actively realizing this relationship.

Numerous different types, models, or applications of small groups can fit within our definition. There is no one right method or type of group. Nevertheless, most groups are able to fit within the general characteristics of this definition.

BIBLICAL GOALS FOR SMALL GROUPS

Later, we'll explore the different types or models of small groups. For now, recognize that different types of groups can have diverse goals (totally different, somewhat the same, shared, overlapping, conflicting, etc.). Goals are the ideals they are trying to accomplish. Nevertheless, let me suggest that *all* types of groups in the church share four basic goals that are foundational to our corporate, over-arching purpose of glorifying God (1 Corinthians 10:31):

◆ Foster biblical love (John 13:35; 1 Corinthians 13:13; Galatians 5:13; Ephesians 5:2; 1 John 4:7,11,21). God is love. This divine characteristic should also be true of those who claim to be in Christ. Remember, biblical love is demonstrated love.

◆ Promote fellowship (koinonia) and unity (Acts 4:32; Romans 12:5; 1 Corinthians 12:12,25; Ephesians 4:3,5,13; 1 John 1:3,6-7). Unity should characterize the fellowship or communion of a community of believers. God is one; likewise, we should be one.

◆ Build the Body (Romans 14:19; Ephesians 2:19-22; 4:11-16; Colossians 1:10-12,28; 2:6-7). Whether it is evangelism or discipleship of believers, the goal is to present all people mature (complete) in Christ.

◆ Nurture spiritual gifts (Romans 12:6-8, 1 Corinthians 12:4-11). Ministry is a shared task—a task for which we are all responsible. Each of us needs to find a suitable expression to exercise his or her spiritual gift(s).

Actually, all of the activities provided by a local church should contribute to some degree to attaining these goals. Nevertheless, of all the legitimate ministry contexts a church can offer, small groups provide one of the most practical and ready platforms to successfully nurture these vital goals. If your small group (regardless of the type) isn't advancing these essentials, a serious reevaluation is in order.

CHAPTER TWO

Seeing Yourself as a Group Leader

W hen you look into a mirror, do you see a group leader? What does a group leader look like? What does that person do?

Rest easy. You needn't be perfect. There is no such thing as the *perfect* group leader. There's no required age, appearance, personality type, or experience—no standardized, insurmountable role embraced by every group leader. The only perfect group leader was Jesus Christ, but *He was God.* The rest of us are imperfect humans. Nevertheless, with the help of the Holy Spirit you can become a terrific group leader. Some basic qualifications and a clear understanding of the task are essential to your success.

Every leadership position within a local church has two fundamental attributes: (1) the qualifications for service, and (2) the specific tasks, or a job description. Serving as a small group leader is no exception. While the specifics of these two attributes can vary from one situation to the next, we will investigate some generic qualifications and role responsibilities. Next we'll examine the ideal leadership style. Finally, we will discuss shared leadership.

QUALIFICATIONS OF A GROUP LEADER

I routinely ask the participants in my small group courses and seminars to list the qualifications a person should have to serve as a group leader. After they have made their lists, which usually are quite long, I ask, "How many people do you know in your church who meet all your criteria?" Typically no one knows anyone who fits the bill perfectly. Immediately I ask my second question: "How many of *you* meet all the criteria?" As expected, everyone quickly concedes that he or she falls short. However, there are some indispensable qualifications every group leader should possess.

An understanding of spiritual principles—The point of 1 Timothy 5:22 is that a new believer should not be given too much responsibility too soon. This is an important principle in selecting small group leaders. You must be a Christian for a sufficient length of time. How long? Some people are ready after one year, others after ten years. The length of time varies with the person, but you need enough time to understand spiritual principles and demonstrate the next qualification.

A growing relationship with Christ—Second Peter 3:18 tells us to "grow in the grace and knowledge of our Lord and Savior Jesus Christ." If you are to model spiritual growth and encourage it in others, it first must be a reality in your own life. Your emerging Christlike character should be evident to all.

A commitment to caring for people—In 1 Corinthians 12:25 we are instructed to "have the same care for one another." The person meeting this standard is dedicated to reaching out to the group members and assisting as needed, comforting them in distressing times, joining them in rejoicing over success, supporting their efforts at self-improvement, and investing time in other activities that express care and concern.

A desire to serve—"Through love serve one another" (Galatians 5:13). Leading is serving, as we shall see in a few moments. The motivation to serve must be deeply rooted in the potential leader. You must be willing to undertake the responsibilities of leading a group.

A willingness to learn—"Trying to learn what is pleasing to the Lord" (Ephesians 5:10) applies to everything you do, including your service as a small group leader. You may not know everything about being a group leader right now, but you must be willing to learn.

A resolve to spend the necessary time—Having the necessary time it takes to lead a group is an important qualification. Leading a small group must "be done properly and in an orderly manner" (1 Corinthians 14:40). Are you willing to spend the time demanded to lead a group?

The above list could be longer. However, these six qualifications are at the center of what it takes to succeed as a small group leader. Any further qualifications you or I might list can fit under one of these six.

I picked up an astute idea somewhere that reduces the six qualifications down to three. The three qualifications are contained in this easily remembered phrase: *F-A-T* people make the best leaders. Let me explain:

F —Faithful to God and your fellow group members.
A —Available, having and being willing to spend the time.
T —Teachable, open to instruction and learning.

What was your reaction after reading these basic qualifications? It's easy to become somewhat discouraged. The standards are high. As I've said, not one of us is perfect. We can be thankful that God doesn't expect us to be perfect. Therefore, while all the qualifications must be present to some degree, each leader will be strong in certain ones and need further improvement in others. The pivotal challenge is allowing the Holy Spirit to help you in your areas of weakness. Like the Apostle Paul, our ultimate success is found in the claim, "I can do all things through Him who strengthens me" (Philippians 4:13).

JOB DESCRIPTION

What does a small group leader do? What is that person's job description?

Before we answer these questions—to get us on the same wavelength and to provide a context for our discussion of the leader's role—I need to define what I mean by "small group leader."

A small group's designated leader is the person(s) appointed and recognized to serve the group by enabling the members to achieve their purpose(s) for being a group.

This definition of a small group leader is broad in scope, but it's very useful in helping to describe the basics of the leadership role. Let me explain the definition in detail, as when we defined *small group,* by examining its various words and phrases.

Designated leader—A healthy group shares leadership. However, most groups also need a specified leader to set the pace and oversee any necessary administrative details. You'll find that some groups have an "undesignated" leader—a person without the title who is in reality the group's process leader. But rarely is this person willing to formally assume the defined role of designated leader. Therefore, the designated leader plays a pivotal role through assisting the group to get launched, establish a heading, and gain momentum. Initially, the designated leader usually serves the group by:

- ◆ Explaining purpose and vision
- ◆ Initiating structure
- ◆ Clarifying expectations
- ◆ Encouraging participation
- ◆ Organizing details

Person(s) appointed and recognized—The role of the designated leader may be undertaken by one person or shared among several. I know of groups led by husband-wife teams and others led by two unrelated friends. The number of leaders isn't as important as the method by which they assume the role. Their appointment may be the result of a vote taken by the group, a default outcome because no one else is willing to serve, or a voluntary undertaking after much prayer and discussion. The latter option is my preferred method.

In every case it is important for the person or persons in leadership to have the full recognition of the group members—and when appropriate, of those leading the overall small groups' ministry. Groups that lack a recognized leader are risking a rocky beginning, an ineffective life, and a hurried conclusion.

To serve the group by enabling the members—The leader is responsible to assist and encourage the group in individual and mutual spiritual growth as an active member of the group, rather than as a detached observer. In doing this, the attitudes and actions of a servant must prevail. A group leader isn't an autocratic boss, but rather an enabler of relationships and process—a servant-leader in a position of caring influence.

To achieve their purpose(s) for being a group—Small groups within the church exist for the members' *mutual* Christian edification and fellowship. Accomplishing this general goal is central to the leader's role. However, groups often have varying specific purposes and goals that guide their existence. Even with this potential variety, the defined task of the leader doesn't change. Leadership carries the responsibility of assisting the group to clarify, pursue, monitor, and achieve its reason(s) for being a group.

Now we are ready to consider specific tasks, or a group leader's job description. Here again, I need to be somewhat general in my prescriptions. Each situation presents unique requirements that need specific applications. However, it is possible to formulate a list of activities or responsibilities common to most group leaders. Many, if not all, of the following tasks will apply to you:

◆ Listening—Being a good listener, really hearing what people have to say.

◆ Leading discussion—Guiding, or teaching others how to guide, effective discussions.

◆ Enabling group decision making—Helping the group make choices at various points in its corporate life.

◆ Understanding and leading group process—Being knowledgeable and skilled in facilitating group dynamics.

◆ Practicing (modeling) openness and caring—Setting the example by being honest, empathetic, and actively seeking ways to assist group members.

◆ Planning and leading group meetings—Preparing for and conducting group sessions, or helping other group members to do so.

◆ Dealing with conflict and problems—Guiding the group to confront and resolve interpersonal strife and general difficulties faced by the group.

◆ Following up the various members outside of group meetings—Expressing concern for members at various times apart from regular meetings.

◆ Attending planning and learning opportunities for group

leaders—When applicable, participating in the training and organizational meetings of any existing larger overall groups' program.
♦ Evaluating progress—Making judgments and decisions about various aspects of the group's existence and accomplishments.

By now you know that I like lists. Even though the next one overlaps with some of the things I've already mentioned, here's someone else's list of basic skills included in the group leader's tasks:

1. *Listen* to others.
2. *Summarize* where the group is.
3. *Ask questions* in specific ways to guide the group in a needed direction.
4. *Cope with conflict* when it arises and/or be willing to elicit a hidden conflict when the group is avoiding it.
5. *Be patient* when the group needs to struggle with an issue (without being rescued by a leader).
6. *Distinguish* between your personal needs as the leader and the needs of the group. (Ask yourself: Am I meeting my needs at the expense of the group?)
7. *Share leadership* functions within the group without being threatened that you will lose control of the group.
8. *Facilitate* one member relating his or her contribution to another's idea in order to keep the discussion "building" in one direction.
9. *Deal* with ideas, tasks, and feelings and develop a sense of timing when the maintenance of the group's life should be given priority over content or task.
10. *Be comfortable* with group silence.
11. *Keep* the group *focused on issues* rather than on members' personalities.
12. Help the group to *solve problems* and *make evaluations.*
13. *Delegate* responsibility.
14. With the group, *work* through *setting goals* and *revising* its goals when necessary.

15. *Enable* the group to *understand* and *learn* from its own group process.
16. *Bring* the group to the point of facing its own need to *terminate* when its task and/or time is completed.[1]

Ideally, if you are part of a larger groups' ministry, you were given or will be given a written job description that incorporates many or all of the items in the two lists you've just read. On the next page you'll find a copy of the job description my church uses. Our groups are called *Caringroups*. Note: (1) this job description isn't long, (2) it stipulates specifics including the amount of time expected, and (3) it includes what the group leader can expect.

A detailed job description is a useful tool. It outlines your specific responsibilities and states the types of assistance you can expect. If you don't have a job description, ask for one. In some cases it may be necessary to write your own and have it approved by the appropriate leader(s) in your situation. Whatever your circumstance, clarifying the details of your role as a group leader is helpful in getting started in the task, monitoring your progress, and avoiding unstated expectations.

Caringroup Leader's Job Description

1. Accept the oversight of a specific caringroup.
2. Facilitate the group's weekly meeting.
3. Lead the group in selecting an appropriate meeting format(s) that is in keeping with the group's goals.
4. Encourage (and model) acceptance, understanding, and sharing among group members.
5. Maintain regular contact with group members and serve as a channel of communication, motivation, and concern between individual group members and the whole group.
6. Follow-up group members who are absent (from the group, worship, or Christian education) to let them know they were missed. When appropriate, assist in finding a way to alleviate the reason for the absence.
7. Attend an initial leadership training workshop and the subsequent group leaders' meetings held every six to eight weeks. (We call

these "STP" meetings—sharing, tips, and prayer.)
8. Serve for a minimum of one year, after approval by the elders, with no maximum time limit.
9. Invest a minimum of two hours per week (excluding meetings) in preparation and group member contacts.
10. Complete and submit a six-month group calendar (two per year) and monthly progress reports on behalf of the group.
11. Seek help when confronted with difficulties.
12. When the group is associated with an adult education class, keep the class leader apprised of group success and needs.
13. Be responsible to a caringroup steering (guidance) committee.

Assistance provided:
◆ Monthly contact from a member of the steering committee
◆ Resource ideas
◆ Training workshop and STP meetings
◆ Other assistance as needed[2]

YOUR LEADERSHIP STYLE

Knowing what is expected of you as a small group leader is indispensable. In turn, how you go about those duties is a related but distinct issue of huge relevance. The attitudes, methods, and behavior that mark you as a leader can be referred to as your *leadership style*. Realizing how you operate—your unique style—is vital. This knowledge can provide feedback for determining your areas of leadership success, as well as assistance in identifying areas of needed improvement.

The Traditional Leader
For many years it has been popular to describe leadership styles in terms of the leader being either autocratic, democratic, or laissez-faire. I'll define these quickly.

The *autocratic* leader dominates the process, makes all the decisions, and generally "owns" the group. Members of the group are not consulted, nor are they perceived by the leader as equal participants. This style of leader demands and gets his or her own way. Objecting members can find a new group.

Leaders who are *democratic* seek the input and participation of all the members. They emphasize hearing all opinions and ideas. Every group member has an equal say in making decisions and is held equally accountable for results.

The *laissez-faire* leader is basically passive. Whatever the group wants is just fine. This type of leader actively avoids confrontation, disagreement, initiating behavior, and asserting personal preferences. In short, it's leadership in name only.

Which style is best? After acknowledging that all three have some usefulness, most people advocate the democratic option. It reflects our sociological idealism: Democracy has served the United States well, so it must be good enough for our churches and small groups. Of course, there is some truth to this line of thinking. But can there be an alternative that approaches the issue from a different angle with a better perspective? I'm sure that you already guessed my answer: yes. In my opinion, the best alternative is the biblical concept of servant-leadership.

The Servant-Leader

Doug Whallon makes a clear distinction in a chapter titled, "Leadership— the Critical Factor," in *Good Things Come in Small Groups*, a book written by the members of a small group. He convincingly points out that the biblical model of leadership is built on twin concepts: (1) a servant serves by leading, and (2) a leader leads by serving. I summarize this idea by referring to the group leader as a *servant-leader.*

On one occasion the Lord Jesus' disciples were discussing which one of them was the greatest. Later, Jesus asked what they had been talking about. The disciples sheepishly admitted their topic. Jesus' response set the standard for then and now, "If anyone wants to be first, he shall be last of all, and servant of all" (Mark 9:35). In other words, among God's people the greatest person is the one who serves the most. Servanthood was established as the genuine, true leadership model.

Jesus modeled servant-leadership. His were more than mere words; He practiced what He taught. The event that so effectively represented the epitome of service in His day was when He washed His disciples' feet (John 13:5). This act of servanthood is even more impressive when you consider He had the right, more than any other human, to demand to be served by those around Him. Jesus was God, yet He voluntarily chose to give up His heavenly prerogatives, take on human form, be born and raised in humble circumstances, live a simple life of service, and ultimately, lay down His life for you and me. *This is servanthood!*

Following the example of the Lord Jesus, the Apostle Paul took on the mantle of servanthood. He openly advocated his role as a servant (some versions use the word *minister*) of these things:

- ◆ Christians in Corinth (1 Corinthians 3:5)
- ◆ New Covenant (2 Corinthians 3:6)
- ◆ God (2 Corinthians 6:4)
- ◆ Christ (2 Corinthians 11:23)
- ◆ Gospel (Colossians 1:23)
- ◆ Church (Colossians 1:25)

Paul sums up his servant's attitude with these words: "For though I am free from all men, I have made myself a slave to all, that I might win the more" (1 Corinthians 9:19). This was an awe-inspiring statement coming from a man who was highly educated and had been a member of the Jewish religious elite. *This is servanthood.*

Our needed response seems obvious. As group leaders, we must embrace the example of Jesus and of Paul—especially if we take seriously Paul's admonition, "Be imitators of me, just as I also am of Christ" (1 Corinthians 11:1).

You'll find that being a servant-leader is difficult. It runs against the grain of our humanness. Servanthood is both frustrating and upsetting at times. Even though it's tough, never forget Peter's words: "Whoever serves, let him do so as by the strength which God supplies" (1 Peter 4:11). *This is servanthood.*

The Situational Leader

Applied servant-leadership within groups requires the practice of what I call "situational leadership." Depending on the stage or phase of group development (discussed in the next chapter), the role of the leader changes. Early in the life of the group, the leader must take an active role in directing, establishing, and maintaining group processes and relationships. As the group finds its identity and unity increases, the leader must reduce the amount of control that was necessary previously and allow the group to be self-directing. Then in the final phase of the group's existence, the leader must once again assert his or her leadership role.

Situational leadership isn't easy. In fact, it is hard at times, because no clear sign posts exist to tell you when the situation requires you to increase or decrease your leadership input. Nevertheless, the probability of your success greatly increases if you (1) remain sensitive to the leading of the Holy Spirit, (2) remember the ideals of servant-leadership, and (3) strike the right balance between the three important dimensions that affect your role as a leader:

- ◆ The dynamics of a group just starting versus one coming to an end
- ◆ The dynamics of people-oriented versus task-oriented processes
- ◆ The dynamics of directive versus passive control

Each dimension operates on a continuum between two extremes. For example, at one end the new group needs a lot of task-oriented decisions, requiring a more directive style of leadership. At the middle of the continuum, most groups require shared leadership that is more passive, because people-oriented processes have become dominant. While at the opposite end of the continuum, the group is ending and the designated leader needs to once again become directive, but not at the same level that was necessary in the beginning.

The three dimensions interact with one another. This means the extremes of any dimension are rarely practiced. The chart below illustrates what I mean. The contrasting conditions are set at opposite ends from one another, but exist with and are overlapped by the other dimensions.

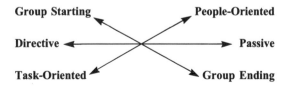

Looking at the chart, try to decide where to put a large dot to represent your group's situation at any given point in time. Where you would put the dot changes from day to day, from task to task, and depending on the length of time the group has met. Doing this little exercise requires you to know about the stages of group development. In the next chapter you'll learn about five stages, which together describe the entire developmental cycle most small groups go through in the course of their existence.

Shared Leadership

You may have the idea that you are responsible for all the leadership tasks within your group. On the contrary, as the designated leader your primary task is to give away the functional leadership of the group. Ideally, the group grows in its development to a point where the members—individually and corporatcly—share the leadership functions. Shared leadership is the ideal for most types of groups in the church. It's an outworking of the unity and functions of the Body of Christ.

I've seen many lists of activities that when practiced would depict the ideal of shared leadership. Here's my list of functional behaviors that exemplify shared leadership and, to be fair, a list of nonfunctional behaviors that hinder or severely damage shared leadership.

Functional behaviors—Certain leadership behaviors strengthen and maintain group viability and effectiveness. Cooperation, mutual support, interdependence, and member satisfaction remain high if the group members individually and corporately share the responsibility for the group's success. The following list contains some of the most important functional, shared leadership behaviors:

◆ Encouraging—Being friendly, warm, responsive to others, praising others and their ideas, agreeing with and accenting contributions of others.
◆ Gate-keeping—Making it possible for another member to make a contribution to the group, or suggesting limited talking time for everyone so that all will have a chance to be heard.
◆ Standard setting—Expressing standards for the group to use

in choosing its content or procedures or in evaluating its decisions, reminding the group to avoid decisions that conflict with group standards.

◆ Following—Going along with decisions of the group, somewhat passively accepting ideas of others, serving as an audience during group discussion and decision making.

◆ Expressing group feelings—Summarizing what group feelings seem to be, describing reactions of the group to ideas or solutions.

◆ Evaluating—Submitting group decisions or accomplishments to comparison with group standards, measuring achievements against goals.

◆ Consensus testing—Tentatively asking for opinions in order to find out if the group is nearing consensus on a decision, tossing ideas around to test group opinions.

◆ Harmonizing—Mediating and conciliating differences in points of view, suggesting compromise solutions.

◆ Tension reducing—Draining off or easing negative feelings by saying calming things or through light jesting, pointing out the wider context of a tense situation.

Nonfunctional behaviors—The following behaviors represent the opposite of shared leadership. They are destructive to the group's success.

◆ Aggression—Working for status by criticizing or blaming others, showing hostility against the group or some person, deflating the ego or status of others.

◆ Blocking—Interfering with the progress of the group by going off on a tangent, citing personal experiences unrelated to the issue, arguing needlessly over a minor point, rejecting ideas without proper consideration.

◆ Self-confessing—Using the group as a sounding board for expressing personal nongroup-oriented feelings or points of view.

◆ Competing—Vying with others to produce the best ideas, talk the most, play the most roles, gain favor with the leader and/or group members.

♦ Seeking sympathy—Trying to induce other group members to a point of view by seeking sympathy to one's problems or misfortunes, degrading one's self or ideas to gain support.

♦ Special pleading—Introducing or supporting suggestions related to one's own pet concerns or philosophies, lobbying.

♦ Horsing around—Clowning, excess joking, mimicking, disrupting the work of the group beyond acceptable levels or group norms.

♦ Recognition seeking—Attempting to call attention to one's self by loud or excessive talking, extreme ideas, or unusual behavior.

♦ Withdrawing—Acting indifferent or passive, resorting to excessive formality, day dreaming, doodling, whispering to others, wandering from the subject, leaving the group activities frequently.

Nonfunctional behaviors usually result when individual needs are not being met by the group. The occurrence of such behavior is a sign that shared leadership hasn't materialized. Group maintenance functions are not being adequately maintained by the group itself or by the designated leader. Obviously, then, our duty as leaders is to help the group avoid these types of behavior and, instead, embrace the functional behaviors of the previous list.

To summarize, I suggest that being a small group leader is:

♦ A willingness and ability to serve others
♦ A function of a group's specific situation
♦ A form of spiritual service best described as servant-leadership
♦ A process of helping group members achieve their common goals
♦ A set of learned (or acquired) skills
♦ An ability to communicate with and motivate others.

NOTES:

1. Adapted from Nathan W. Turner, *Effective Leadership in Small Groups* (Valley Forge: Judson Press, 1977).

2. Provided by Emmanuel Community Church, Clackamas, Oregon.

CHAPTER THREE

Understanding Your Group's Development

S mall groups are like people. Every group goes through identifiable, systematic phases of development or stages of "growing up." Each group develops over a period of time, formulating its unique identity and personality.

The human development or "body" analogy is pictured frequently by the Apostle Paul in the New Testament. For example, he referred to the church as the "body of Christ" (Ephesians 4:12). Speaking about our spiritual development, he said, "When I was a child, I used to speak as a child, think as a child, reason as a child; when I became a man, I did away with childish things" (1 Corinthians 13:11). The human development metaphor effectively communicates spiritual truth.

How often do we speak of infancy, childhood, adolescence, young adulthood, middle age, and old age as phases of human life? The words we use to describe these phases are useful in describing small group development. From conception through adulthood and old age, group development closely models the phases of human growth. This makes sense because a group is made up of people.

Why is a working knowledge of group development important to you? First, it will assist you in nurturing your group's development. Rather than ignorantly watching your group unfold and mature haphazardly, you can actively nurture the process toward mutually beneficial outcomes. Second, knowledge about group development is a practical tool in helping you face or avoid many pitfalls and potential headaches. Being forewarned takes the edge off the shock when a problem does appear and prepares you to handle the situation.

THE SMALL GROUP LIFE CYCLE

Phase One—Birth and Infancy (Forming)

The first phase of a group's life cycle begins before the group ever meets, when the initial idea to start a group is conceived. The "genes" come from a union of the vision and the context that nurtured the decision to create a group by inviting people to participate. Moreover, a group's potential success is intimately linked to the conditions under which it was conceived and must exist. Nurturing environments usually produce healthy, well-adjusted groups. Conversely, neglectful or stressful "birth" environments often yield problem groups. The importance of proper care during a "pre-natal" period cannot be over stressed.

A group can be an "only child" or part of a larger family of groups, but each one is a unique entity, possessing a distinct identity and personality. Immediately following birth, the first vestiges of this uniqueness begin to appear. The mix of ideas and personalities represented in the group create a group personality.

The birth and infancy phase is characterized by initiating and by tentative actions. Each new experience sets the tone for future actions or responses. It is necessary for the leader(s) to provide clear explanations of why the group exists, the format and agenda (or options, if the group is to make these decisions), and other details. When members learn names and particulars of one another it helps them assess their own comfort level within the group. First impressions have a strong effect, and even if incorrect, they are difficult to erase.

The group members come to the first meeting with a certain amount of hesitancy, especially those who have never been in a small group before. Here are some of the questions going through their minds: Will I fit? Who else is in the group? Do I feel comfortable with these people? What is the group going to do? What is going to be expected of me? Can I trust these people?

During this first phase the group is highly dependent on the leader—like a newborn child is dependent on his mother. As the leader you'll need to show a lot of initiative.

One or more of your group members may drop out at this early stage, because they don't feel comfortable with the direction of the group or their initial experience. Be sure to clarify the reasons, but don't twist anyone's arm to remain in the group.

Although this first phase is short, it demands that you provide certain information and processes that are vital to the formation of your group and its success. Here are the key leadership issues of the first phase:

- ◆ Assuring the careful formulation of the group
- ◆ Coordinating the first meeting
- ◆ Clarifying the purpose(s) of the group
- ◆ Providing the opportunity for each member to tell his or her story (name, background, occupation, spiritual journey)
- ◆ Dealing with each member's expectations for the group
- ◆ Helping members feel like they belong
- ◆ Facilitating location and agenda details
- ◆ Introducing format options (if the group selects the format).

Phase Two—Childhood (Norming)

Children are notorious for testing to see how much they can get away with. While the adults in your group are not children, this same type of testing takes place during the childhood phase of group development. The members are learning what is and isn't acceptable, how and how not to behave, what is and isn't permissible, and what is and isn't expected of group members. We'll call this process of learning the boundaries *norming*. Every group has norms, spoken or unspoken.

Children and groups can be left on their own to grow up by chance. However, like a good parent, you'll do well to systematically plan for and guide the norming process. This means budgeting group time for discussing the establishment and practice of mutually acceptable group norms—standards to govern your group.

The childhood phase provides the first facets of group identity building. In reflecting group norms, the members are beginning to see themselves as a group. Individualism is giving way to group identity and well-being. The personal pronoun *I* is less frequent in favor of *us.* Group members begin to refer to the group as *our* group, and one step further, start referring to it as *my* group.

A certain amount of "storming" is inevitable. Establishing norms can be difficult, or at least confusing. Strong-willed members may insist on their way and create resentment among others. Control of the group is at stake. But with the right leadership on your part, these same people can turn the corner, accept mutual norms, and become fiercely loyal group members.

An excellent tool to assist your group through its childhood phase, and prepare for maturity, is a *covenant.* Just as the name implies, a covenant is an agreement entered into by the group members—a pledge to uphold certain standards and expectations. Simply stated, a covenant outlines the group norms. My preference is a written covenant, but it can be merely a verbal agreement.

On pages 46-48 you'll find a copy of the covenant my group uses. I originally presented it as a tentative suggestion. The group members were free to add or subtract items as they wished. We spent two sessions going over the items and talking about what each one meant and how it would affect us individually and corporately. After agreeing that we would accept the covenant, and coming to the understanding that it would not be a club used against anyone, we each signed a copy of the document and kept it for our own reference. There is something about signing a document that seals the terms in our hearts and minds.

Before we go on, here are the main leadership issues of the second phase:

- Clarifying members expectations for the group
- Assisting the members in becoming a group
- Discussing group norms
- Affirming individual participation
- Helping to resolve initial conflict
- Establishing a group covenant (or written equivalent)
- Deciding on a group format (if appropriate).

Caringroup Covenant

Caringroups are a *key* method in helping us experience the relationships and the fellowship necessary within the Body of Christ. Genuine biblical fellowship *is possible,* with God's help through our individual and mutual commitment. To assist us as group members in achieving the goals of identification, love, caring, and accountability to God, and to guide us in our mutual commitment to one another as brothers and sisters in Jesus Christ, the following covenants are set forth:

The Covenant of Affirmation and Acceptance:
I pledge to accept you no matter what you have done, are doing, or will do. I may not agree with your every action, but I will attempt to love you as a child of God and do all I can to express God's affirming love. I need you.

The Covenant of Availability:
Everything I have—time, energy, insight, possessions—is at your disposal if you have a need . . . to the limit of my resources. As part of this availability, I pledge to meet with you in this group on a regular basis.

The Covenant of Prayer:
I promise to pray for you regularly.

The Covenant of Honesty:
I agree to strive to become a more open and honest person, to share my true opinions, feelings, struggles, joys, and hurts . . . as well as I am able. I will trust you with my dreams and problems.

The Covenant of Feedback:
I will attempt to mirror back to you what I am hearing you say and what you are feeling. If this means risking pain for either of us, I will trust our relationship enough to take the risk, realizing it is in "speaking the truth in love that we grow up in every way into Christ who is the head" (Ephesians 4:15). I will try to express this feedback in a sensitive and controlled manner, in keeping with the circumstances.

The Covenant of Sensitivity:
Even as I desire to be known and understood by you, I pledge to be sensitive to you and your needs to the best of my ability. I will try to

hear you, see your point of view, understand your feelings, and draw you out of possible discouragement or withdrawal.

The Covenant of Confidentiality:
I promise to keep whatever is shared within the confines of this group. I vow to not push you to share things about yourself that you would prefer to keep undisclosed.

In full acceptance of these covenants, I affix my name to this document in recognition of my commitment to God and the members of this caringroup. I will keep this document as a reminder of this voluntary covenant, which I've entered into on this date.

_____   _____
Signature   Date

Phase Three—Teenage (Conforming)
Every teenager goes through a time of questioning and conforming. Likewise, groups moving from childhood to maturity can expect to go through a "teenage" period. At times it's a rocky road. Other times a group may move through this phase almost without noticing.

The group's transition into the teenage phase isn't marked by some momentous event, such as a thirteenth birthday. However, at this point, your group has been meeting for approximately ten weeks—two and one-half months. The conforming phase is a time of transition. Becoming a mature group is very close. All the infancy and childhood issues should have been addressed and the group's identity is nearly complete.

Questioning and adjustment are the two major events in this third phase. It's natural to question. By this point in the group's life the members are beginning to feel free to call into question corporate decisions and practices. Some of the initial inhibitions are gone. Voicing agreement or disagreement with relationships and activities is easier, and so may happen. Don't be surprised if everything seems to be going along well, then suddenly one or two members begin to question and/or complain about various aspects of the group.

How you as the leader react to this questioning directly affects the group's future. You must recognize that in most cases it is a healthy step in the group's development. On a rare occasion the motivation behind the dissatisfaction is less than honorable. But in any case, you must work through the questions by honestly address-ing the issues. Remember to relax, be reasonable, involve the group members, and seek to honor Jesus Christ. Your goal is to help the group take responsibility for itself. In doing so, you actively support the group's continuing growth and development. Failure to do so may derail the group.

Major or minor adjustments may be necessary. A change in schedule, altering the format, or time spent working through some relational issue are examples of potential realignments. Some group leaders think that it reflects poorly on them if they allow the group to make any changes. Just the opposite is true; making changes is okay. To assist you, you'll find that formative evaluation—a topic we'll discuss in the last chapter—provides excellent tools to work through this questioning and adjustment process.

Once the group has worked through its teenage problems, the members are ready to begin functioning like a group, to enjoy the fruit of their efforts. This maturity is described in the next phase. These are the key leadership issues to remember for phase three:

* Allowing the members to question the group practices
* Accepting the need to make adjustments
* Conducting formative evaluation (discussed in chapter 7)
* Helping the group accept responsibility for itself
* Adjusting where adjustment is needed
* Affirming group involvement in decision making.

Phase Four—Maturity (Performing)

The fourth phase of group development portrays the mature func-tioning of the group. Now the group is really clicking. The purpose for which it exists is being realized. Whether your group is process-oriented, content-oriented, task-oriented, or need-oriented (see chap-ter 4), the group views itself as being successful. Lord willing, the maturity phase will be the longest phase of your group's life.

A major leadership task during this phase is to work with the group in maintaining the interpersonal relationships and processes stipulated in your covenant. Ideally, maintaining these aspects of your group's life has become a shared process. Everyone in the group is taking the responsibility. Nevertheless, conscious and deliberate steps must be taken to monitor the covenant dynamics and procedural details. Doing so assures continuing vitality.

As all adults have ups and downs in their personal lives, groups also experience highs and lows. Every group meeting won't be fantastic. You'll have bad days. I remember several group meetings that were so bad they became jokes among my fellow group members. We frequently kidded each other about those meetings. This was possible because the relationships among the members were strong, and we all realized no one and no group was perfect.

Be alert. After more than just one or two poor meetings, some groups experience a "mid-life crisis." Boredom with the routine, unresolved conflicts, ambiguous norms, conflicting schedules, lack of variety, and so on, could all trigger this affliction. When this type of crisis occurs, extra effort is needed to identify the cause and seek its satisfactory resolution. Not every group, however, will experience a mid-life crisis. Many groups sail through the maturity phase unscathed.

Evaluation and adjustment once again are important considerations. The mature group must not rest on its success. A continuing emphasis on formative evaluation, a continual testing of the atmosphere, is always a good idea. Not that you are trying to find problems that don't exist, but evaluation reflects an openness to improvement.

On occasion, groups aren't successful in moving through the preliminary phases prerequisite to the mature phase of group existence. They never grow up. This means they usually end up disbanding, for whatever reason. I will talk more about the reasons why groups terminate toward the end of this chapter.

The key leadership issues for the fourth phase are these:

- ◆ Maintaining group relationships, procedures, and details
- ◆ Encouraging continued participation
- ◆ Helping the group to be responsible for itself
- ◆ Assisting the group to deal with the ups and downs
- ◆ Conducting a formative evaluation
- ◆ Making necessary adjustment for improvement.

Phase Five—Old Age and Demise (Reforming)

A mature, successful group doesn't conclude on its last meeting. Actually, the process takes place over a number of the final meetings. Demise is a process. You are dealing with a group that has overcome dying from a "heart attack" or other small group disease, and now is ending due to natural causes.

The old age phase can happen by design or by default. As is the case with most issues in growing successful groups, we make choices and decisions that affect what we do and how we do it. Some groups are planned to last for a specific amount of time. Others begin with no such stipulation and continue until a good reason for ending presents itself. In either case, the final phase in the course of a group's life must not be overlooked. Careful attention must be given to ending the group on a positive note and paving the way for the members' future involvement in groups.

As the group leader, increased initiative on your part is needed. Helping the group through this phase means once again—as in the beginning—playing a more assertive role. As the leader you must assume the role of helping the members deal openly and honestly with the positive, and perhaps negative, feelings associated with group termination.

Dealing with the "grief process" associated with termination is important. Many groups are so successful it is very hard for them to disband. They view termination as if it meant the group was a potential murder victim. Some groups don't want the demise to happen and, consequently, choose to continue.

However, if your situation requires groups to conclude and reform on a scheduled basis, it is vital that you help the members understand the value inherent in this process. The strong relationships that have developed needn't be severed. Instead, the members have the opportunity to experience the joy of making new friends among the Body of Christ. Therefore, the grief process needs to be refocused into a time of reflection and celebration.

Reflecting on and celebrating the struggles and successes experienced by the group during its lifetime is a vital element in this final phase. One or two of the final meetings should be dedicated to this theme. Laugh and cry together. Enjoy your reminiscing. Praise God for each other and the group as a whole.

Summative evaluation is another important final activity your group must accomplish. Here I am referring to a formal process of gathering specific information to be used to make judgments and decisions about the group. This process is indispensable. It provides the basis for capitalizing on group achievements, while avoiding the tendency to repeat mistakes. Chapter 7 goes into depth on the topic of evaluation.

Finally, remember that phase five paves the way for future groups. Working through it successfully is a key in setting the tone and facilitating the success of the groups that will come after you. These will be the key leadership issues during this fifth phase:

◆ Recognizing the dynamics of group termination
◆ Assisting the group to understand and deal with ending
◆ Facilitating reflection and celebration
◆ Paving the way for new groups
◆ Conducting summative evaluation
◆ Completing any final administrative tasks.

A good question at this point is, "How long does each phase last?" Estimating the number of group sessions per phase is a difficult but useful undertaking. Difficult because every group is unique, useful because the time estimates provide working guidelines to assist you in planning and evaluating your group. On page 53 is a summary chart that outlines the average number of group meetings it takes to move through each of the five phases. These estimates (they are only estimates) describe the group that meets for one year—forty-eight sessions. Groups that meet for less than one year and/or less than once per week may not fit the estimates. Likewise, some groups whiz through the initial phases and enjoy a mature existence for the majority of the time they are together. This often happens when the members have had previous positive group experiences.

One final observation about the phases of group development before moving on to our next subject: You may find it helpful to describe the five phases to your group members to prepare them to work through some of the issues. However, I suggest you not make it a topic of extended discussion. Dwelling on these generalizations may actually have a negative result. False ideas about and/or expectations for the group could result. Your members may lose sight of the idea that the phases are only generalizations and expect, maybe even demand, to address every potential issue we've discussed. So in summary, the phases are descriptions of stages most groups go through in becoming a group. They are generalizations, not requirements.

Phase One—Birth and Infancy (Forming)
two to three sessions
Phase Two—Childhood (Norming)
six to seven sessions
Phase Three—Teenage (Conforming)
five to six sessions
Phase Four—Maturity (Performing)
thirty sessions
Phase Five—Old Age and Demise (Reforming)
five to six sessions

CHARACTERISTICS OF ALL GROUPS

Let's take a wide perspective for a few minutes. You'll find it helpful in understanding your group to know about certain dimensions or characteristics all groups possess. Every group must deal with the ten issues you are about to discover. We can and will present each dimension separately, but in reality, they are interrelated and affect each other. Please keep this in mind.

Let me quickly identify the characteristics and list some representative questions to guide your thinking about your own group.

Background—The sum total of experiences and expectations brought to the group by its members.

◆ To what extent are members prepared to enter the group?
◆ What is the history, if any, of the group?
◆ What expectations do group members have about their participation?
◆ Is there a positive history of small groups in the church or organization?
◆ What kind of people compose the group?

◆ Do members have previous experience with small groups?
◆ How were members invited to participate in the group?
◆ What arrangements have been made for group meetings?
◆ How does the small group fit into the scheme of a larger
groups' ministry?

Participation pattern—The frequency and level of interaction
among the members and participation in the group's activities.

◆ How much of the talking is done by the leader?
◆ How much of the talking is done by group members?
◆ Do members feel free to participate?
◆ To whom are questions or comments usually addressed?
◆ Is participation balanced among the group members?
◆ Do quiet members appear alert and interested?
◆ Are members forced to verbally respond?

Communication—The verbal and nonverbal exchange of information, ideas, and feeling among the group members.

◆ Do members express their ideas clearly?
◆ What types of nonverbal communication are taking place?
◆ Is there freedom to express honest feelings and values?
◆ Do members pick up on ideas and build on them?
◆ Are responses to statements often irrelevant?
◆ Do members feel free to ask for clarification?
◆ Are efforts made to listen carefully when someone else is
speaking?
◆ What marks the communication as being Christlike?

Cohesion—The degree to which members are motivated to
remain in the group.

◆ Does the group work well together as a unit?
◆ Are phrases such as "we" and "our group" used often?
◆ What subgroups or "lone wolves" exist? How do they affect
the group?
◆ Are members seeking to spend additional time together out-
side group meetings?

♦ What level of interest is expressed in group tasks?
♦ Do members often speak of group termination?
♦ Is biblical unity characteristic of the group?

Atmosphere—The spiritual, social, and emotional environment that exists within the group.

♦ What social climate is characteristic of the group?
♦ Would the group be described as relaxed or tense?
♦ Are members friendly or hostile to one another?
♦ Are group meetings formal or informal?
♦ Do members feel free or inhibited in their participation?
♦ Can opposing views or negative feelings be expressed?
♦ How is the love of Christ evidenced among members?

Norms—The standards that govern the individual and corporate behavior of the group members.

♦ Do members understand and accept group norms?
♦ What is the code of ethics governing the group?
♦ Are there deviations from accepted standards? By whom, and how are norms enforced?
♦ Do members perceive that they may set and/or change group norms?
♦ Are group standards in keeping with group goals?
♦ What is the biblical basis for group standards?

Sociometric pattern—The social patterns among group members that emphasize attitudes and actions reflecting acceptance or rejection.

♦ Which members tend to identify and support one another?
♦ Have members labeled each other?
♦ Are group members from different social backgrounds?
♦ Which members seem repeatedly at odds with each other?
♦ What known "like" and "dislike" relationships exist?

◆ To what extent do members have the same care for one another?

Structure and organization—The formulation and arrangement of the group's composition and operation.

◆ How is the group organized to function?
◆ Is the structure understood and accepted by each of the members?
◆ Is the structure appropriate to the group's purpose and tasks?
◆ How does the group relate to other organizations or structures?
◆ What, if any, "invisible" structures exist?
◆ By whom and how are structural and/or organization decisions made?
◆ How are structure and organization inhibiting or promoting group success?

Procedures—The methods by which the group operates.

◆ How does the group determine its tasks and/or its agenda?
◆ By what method does the group make decisions?
◆ How are various members assigned tasks?
◆ How does the group coordinate its various members and activities?
◆ How and on what basis is the group evaluated?
◆ Are accepted procedures known by all group members?
◆ Are group tasks and meetings done in decent and proper order?

Goals—Those purposes or reasons for which the group exists.

◆ Do group members clearly understand why the group exists?
◆ How does the group arrive at its goals?
◆ Are the goals clearly defined?

◆ Are the goals in keeping with the intended purpose or type of group?

◆ Are group goals known by group members?

◆ Do members express commitment to the goals?

◆ Do the goals reflect biblical ideals?

PRACTICAL PRINCIPLES

Over the years a number of time-tested group principles have emerged. They present us with very useful generalizations (not rules) about group members. Your group may differ from these findings, and that is okay. Remember, your group and its members are unique. Yet, having the following generalizations in mind can help you in planning for and ministering to your group.

Principle 1: People join groups in order to satisfy some individual need. A person's primary motivation for small group membership is usually self-centered.

Principle 2: A person will remain in (or join) a small group if he finds the group's goals and activities attractive and rewarding. People base their participation on personal standards.

Principle 3: People prefer to participate in groups where other members are similar in age, attractiveness, attitudes, personality, economic status, perceived ability, and needs.

Principle 4: Total overall participation in a small group decreases with increasing group size. The larger the group, the less its individual members participate in the discussion, activities, and so on.

Principle 5: Group members usually evaluate smaller groups more positively than larger groups.

Principle 6: The smaller the group, the greater the feasibility of shared leadership. Increasing group size increases the probability of a focused leader rather than shared leadership.

Principle 7: The physical setting in which the group meets affects members' attitudes and actions and, consequently, helps determine group process. The meeting place either positively or negatively influences members' participation in the group.

Principle 8: A more socially and personally adjusted group member contributes to effective group functioning, while an unconventional or anxious member inhibits group functioning. A person's level of social and psychological adjustment directly affects the group process.

Principle 9: Individuals who have been Christians a long time contribute no more to the success of the group process than do new believers (but long-time Christians may have an indirect effect on other dimensions).

Principle 10: The spiritually sensitive group member contributes to the functioning of the group, while those claiming or projecting spiritual superiority inhibit group functioning. "Super saints" tend to cause dysfunctional groups.

Principle 11: Members are more highly motivated and perform more efficiently when the group possesses clear goals and an understanding of what must be done to accomplish the goals. Knowing why the group exists and how it achieves purposes stimulates higher levels of participation.

Principle 12: Interpersonal relations are generally more positive in situations where goals are mutually derived and accepted. Shared ownership of goals builds positive interaction among the members.

Principle 13: Group performance is facilitated to the extent that members can freely communicate their feelings of satisfaction with the group's progress toward goals. Successful groups talk about and assess their goal achievement.

Principle 14: Groups whose members are heterogeneous with respect to sex and personality types are more conforming and perform more effectively than groups that are homogeneous with respect to these characteristics. The opposite is true for age. Diversity among the members in some areas is helpful to the group's success.

Principle 15: A high-status group member (such as a pastor) both initiates and receives more communications and may deviate from group norms without being sanctioned if he contributes to the group's goals. Deference usually is afforded to group members who are perceived as important by the other members.

Principle 16: Greater conformity with group norms occurs in groups with decentralized leadership. When the group members share the responsibility for leadership it promotes compliance with group norms.[1]

I think these generalizations explain themselves fairly well. Observing these dynamics can save you from a headache or two. If not, you need to read the next section very carefully.

WHY GROUPS TERMINATE

All groups come to an end. Some for good reasons, many for neutral reasons, and others for undesirable reasons. Rarely is there one single cause. Here are the ten most common grounds for group termination.

The stated length of time expires. This is the ideal reason for a group disbanding, especially those groups that began with a clearly defined time span for existence. However, a set time may not be the ideal reason to end a task- or content-oriented group. (More on the orientation of groups in chapter 4.) An agreement to continue might be needed.

The task is accomplished. Rarely is the "task" (relationships) completed in process- or need-oriented groups. The ending of content- and task-oriented groups, on the other hand, easily fits into this reason.

The group explodes in conflict. When this happens it is bad news. And if it happens, customarily conflict occurs fairly early in a group's life.

A covenant has not been secured. Lacking group norms, the attendance and behavior of the group members disintegrates to the point where all agree that continuance is fruitless.

A conscious decision is made to terminate, for whatever reason. This is a logical choice on the part of the group members. Schedule conflicts, members moving out of town, the desire to try something new, or reformation of the group are all examples of reasons why groups choose to terminate while still on friendly ground.

Group leadership is not sufficient or not matched to the agenda of the group. This is hard on us as leaders. Yet, at times, we may be in over our heads. Task-, need-, and content-oriented groups are susceptible to leadership failure. Process-oriented groups are as well, but because of their very nature, they tend to be more forgiving of inadequate designated leaders.

The group divides to form two new groups. Some churches split groups when they reach a certain size and form smaller new groups. (Caution: This works well only in a limited number of situations.)

Poor administration (time, place, frequency, scheduling) causes members to give up and not participate. In my opinion, there is no good excuse for this happening. Poor administration is normally a result of insufficient leadership.

Conflict with other church programs. Competition between activities is very common in most churches. Group members are forced to choose between group attendance or participation in something else. This situation is indicative of a poor philosophy of ministry—one that sees groups as just another programmatic option.

Members are not compatible. This causes termination to be a logical choice, not necessarily fueled by conflict. One group I'm familiar with had members at both ends of the adult age span. They liked each other, but their interests and needs were too dissimilar. After giving it the old college try for several months, the members realized they were just kidding themselves and disbanded. Then they all joined other groups.

EFFECTIVE GROUPS

Let's end this chapter by making comparisons between effective and ineffective groups. One of the best such comparisons I've come across, even though it isn't directly focused on groups within the church, is this one done by Johnson and Johnson.

Comparison of Effective and Ineffective Groups

Effective Groups	*Ineffective Groups*
◆ Goals are clarified and changed so that the best possible match between individual goals and the group's goals may be achieved; goals are cooperatively structured.	◆ Members accept imposed goals; goals are competitively structured.
◆ Communication is two way, and the open and accurate expression of both ideas and feelings is emphasized.	◆ Communication is one-way and only ideas are expressed; feelings are suppressed or ignored.

Effective Groups

♦ Participation and leadership are distributed among all group members; goal accomplishment, internal maintenance, and developmental change are underscored.

♦ Ability and information determine influence and power, contracts are built to make sure individuals' goals and needs are fulfilled; power is equalized and shared.

♦ Decision-making procedures are matched with the situation; different methods are used at different times; consensus is sought for important decisions; involvement and group discussions are encouraged.

♦ Controversy and conflict are seen as a positive key to members' involvement, the quality and originality of decisions, and the continuance of the group in good working condition.

♦ Interpersonal, group, and intergroup behaviors are stressed; cohesion is advanced through high levels of inclusion, affection, acceptance, support, and trust. Individuality is endorsed.

Ineffective Groups

♦ Leadership is delegated and based upon authority; membership participation is unequal, with high-authority members dominating; only goal accomplishment is emphasized.

♦ Position determines influence and power; power is concentrated in the authority positions; obedience to authority is the rule.

♦ Decisions are always made by the highest authority; there is little group discussion; members' involvement is minimal.

♦ Controversy and conflict are ignored, denied, avoided, or suppressed.

♦ The functions performed by members are emphasized; cohesion is ignored and members are controlled by force. Rigid conformity is promoted.

Effective Groups

♦ Problem-solving adequacy is high.

♦ Members evaluate the effectiveness of the group and decide how to improve its functioning; goal accomplishment, internal maintenance, and development are all considered important.

Ineffective Groups

♦ Problem-solving adequacy is low.

♦ The highest authority evaluates the group's effectiveness and decides how goal accomplishment may be improved; internal maintenance and development are ignored as much as possible; stability is affirmed.[2]

NOTES:
1. These principles were adapted from Marvin E. Shaw, *Group Dynamics: The Psychology of Small Group Behavior* (New York: McGraw-Hill, 1981).
2. D. W. Johnson and F. P. Johnson, *Joining Together: Group Theory and Group Skills,* Third Edition (Englewood Cliffs, N. J.: Prentice-Hall, 1987), page 11. Reprinted by permission of Prentice Hall, Inc., Englewood Cliffs, New Jersey.

CHAPTER FOUR

Knowing Your Group

K nowing your group—both the individual members and the corporate entity—is a major responsibility of group leadership.
Every small group has a unique personality, a set of distinctive characteristics that make it different from other groups. Yet, despite their
diversity, all groups share some things in common. This commonality
affects the internal and external functioning of a group and is reflected
in three areas.

First, every group has a *purpose for existing,* a reason for being
a group. Numerous reasons are possible, but most groups fit into
one of four broad categories or types. Within these types the specific
goals and objectives may be short-term and functional, or long-term
and spiritual. The goals may be clearly stated or assumed, high and
lofty or narrow and mundane. Yet in every case, the group's type and
purpose must be recognized and monitored if it is to be successful.
Consequently, leading a group involves clarifying the type of group
it is and determining its goals and objectives.

Second, all small groups are *organized* to some degree. The
amount of organization may be slight or highly detailed. The group's
structure and organization are usually direct reflections of the size and
amount of organization that exists within the larger group that spon-
sors the small group's existence and operation. The organizational
options range from loosely associated independent groups to highly
controlled groups that are part of a ministry sponsored by a church
or agency.

Third, and most important, small groups are a human activity. People make up groups; groups exist to serve people. As such, our mutual humanness sets into motion inherent group characteristics, innate qualities that reflect the motivation, ideas, and personal qualities of members. The wise group leader tunes in to these characteristics and makes every effort to know and understand the members of his or her group.

To help you gain a better understanding of the factors involved in knowing your group, let's consider these three areas of commonality in greater detail. I'll ask and then answer some questions to help clarify the concepts you must deal with. We'll start by considering the purpose of your group. Next we'll consider your group's format. Then we'll discuss the most important aspect of your group, the members. And to conclude the chapter, I've provided a situation checklist to help you clarify the characteristics and conditions under which your group operates.

KNOW YOUR GROUP'S PURPOSE

The governing principle that sets the standard for everything we do as Christians, individually or corporately, is stated in 1 Corinthians 10:31—"in whatever you do, do all to the glory of God."

These words, penned by the Apostle Paul, are foundational to any group ministry. Yet, based on this general directive, it is possible to identify specific goals and objectives to guide your group. These guideposts are normally a product of the type of group you are leading. Here are questions to help you think through the type and purpose of your group.

What "Type" of Group Are You Leading?

It seems every author on the topic of small groups has his or her list of types of small groups. Most lists are based on a description of the group's *main* activity. For example, study groups, discussion groups, support groups, fellowship groups, or evangelism groups are a few of the more common types. Such lists are good, but let me offer my alternative.

Before deciding on the specific activity or activities a group will undertake, I've found it useful to determine the thrust or *primary focus* of the group, the central reason for which the group exists. Over the years this approach has led me to identify four basic types of groups.

Process-oriented groups—This type of group focuses on being a group. That is, the central focus is on the spiritual and/or social relationships among the members. What the group does—its meeting format—is a secondary issue. Emphasis is placed on group identity, the dynamics of relationships, and the processes necessary to bring these about. Terms such as "growth group," "caring group," "support group," or "covenant group" are often used to describe this type of group orientation.

Content-oriented groups—This classification includes a variety of Bible study and discussion groups. The main reason for meeting is to study or discuss a biblical passage or topic of mutual relevance. Interpersonal relationships are of concern but normally are assumed. Little if any time is spent dealing with group dynamics. The primary focus is on the content.

Task-oriented groups—These are "doing" groups. The primary thrust is to accomplish a defined task, job, or assignment, which the members do together. What the group plans to do—its purpose for meeting—is why the group exists. Relationships among the members take a secondary role and are usually not discussed unless a problem arises. Most committees and planning groups fit into this category. Evangelism groups could also be classified as being task-oriented, although building relationships with unbelievers and modeling relations with believers are part of the task.

Need-oriented groups—The primary reason underlying this type of group is a common need among the members. Sometimes called support groups or recovery groups, the members meet together for common encouragement and understanding. The attitude and actions of the group members say, "I understand your struggle, I've been there myself." Recovering alcoholics, parents of gay children, battered women, or divorced singles are examples of possible members of need-oriented groups.

It is useful to keep these four orientation categories in mind. While a specific group may incorporate various activities, nevertheless, it's fairly simple to identify which of the four types *best* describes the group—its primary focus or the central reason why the group exists. Furthermore, no one type of group is best. All serve a purpose and can be effective. Some churches elect to have only one type, such as process- or content-oriented groups. But with increasing frequency, larger churches are offering all four types.

What Are the Goals and Objectives for Your Group?
The specific goals and objectives that guide an individual group or an overall groups' ministry are inseparably related to group type. Said another way, certain types of groups lend themselves to accomplishing certain kinds of goals and objectives. In chapter 1, you were introduced to general goals that are applicable to all small groups. In addition to these, it is a good idea for a group to set specific objectives to guide it. Ask yourself and your group members: What is it we want to accomplish in our group?

Whole volumes have been written on the subject of goals and objectives. You're wise to pick up a book on the subject to assist you in identifying and *writing down* your statements of purpose. In doing so, be sure to set objectives that are in keeping with your group's type or orientation.

How Does Your Group Fit into the Life of Your Church?
An integral part of knowing the purpose of your group is clarifying how it fits into the general life of your church. More and more churches are making groups an indispensable component of their identity, programming, and function.

Ideally, your group is one of many groups offered by your church. If this is true, it is very likely that many of the issues we are exploring in this book have already been thought through for you. Be sure to clarify the specifics and understand how your group, and you as a leader, fit into the overall picture.

Unfortunately, most churches still view groups as one of the many options on their programmatic smorgasbord. Groups often must compete for the members' attention and participation. It's frequently the case that groups aren't discouraged, they're just not encouraged. No clear rationale clarifies how small groups fit into the church's life and purposes. If this is the situation you find yourself in, don't despair. First, make sure you are convinced of the importance of small groups. Second, work hard to make your individual group a worthwhile experience for the members. Third, seek the right opportunities to share your ideas about the importance of groups. And be patient and wait on the Lord to move in the hearts and minds of your church colleagues.

Having identified the purpose of your group, now you need to turn your attention to the specific format options that are possible.

KNOW YOUR GROUP'S FORMAT

The term *format* refers to what the group does when it meets and the various details necessary to facilitate the meetings. At issue are those familiar questions: What? When? Where? Each of these factors are best answered based on your particular context. Some groups start with all the aspects of the format already decided, others must make these decisions for themselves. Here are common format questions you must resolve.

When Do You Meet?

If the day and time of your meetings are open, you have a wide set of alternatives from which to select. The best day and time are those that assure maximum participation. I've talked with many people who wanted to be in a group but were unable to do so because of a conflict between their schedule and the group's meeting schedule. Some churches get around this potential difficulty by offering groups on a mix of days and times.

If 6:30 a.m. on Monday mornings is best, so be it. There is no right day or perfect time for all groups. These decisions need to be based on the needs of your members. In general, evenings other than Friday or Saturday seem to work best.

Some churches elect to have all their groups meet on a specific day(s) and time(s). This option has some drawbacks, such as the potential of eliminating people who cannot attend at the specified time. It is attractive in situations where (1) all the adults are employed in a similar business or industry, (2) a high degree of group guidance (control) is desired by the church leadership, (3) the group meetings have replaced a traditional meeting such as a "prayer meeting," and/or (4) a quality program is offered at the church facilities for children, permitting the parents to attend a group.

Where Do You Meet?

The ideal location for group meetings is in a home. It can be the group leader's home or that of one of the other members. Many groups like to rotate among all the members' homes. One caution if you select this alternative: you risk confusion and poor attendance. If you still want to have meetings in more than one location, try rotating no more than once per month (assuming you meet weekly), and be sure to publish a schedule.

Some groups have found it ideal for their purposes to meet in restaurants. This works well for early morning breakfast or lunch meetings with working adults. Many restaurants have private rooms you can reserve ahead of time.

On occasion—such as in rural contexts where distances separate the group members—it may be necessary to meet in the church building. If this is the case, try to create an informal atmosphere. Set aside one room and furnish it similar to a living room in a home. In general, do whatever is needed to create an informal, relaxed atmosphere.

How Long Do You Meet?

Two answers to this question are possible. First, determine the amount of time to be budgeted for each meeting. I recommend one-and-a-half to two hours. Your situation may require more or less than this standard, but you'll have the best results if you stick to this ideal time frame.

The members of my group kid me because I'm a stickler about time. I religiously begin and end our sessions on the agreed upon times, reminding them that their time is my stewardship. Even though we officially end on time, rarely do people leave immediately. Those who must go feel free to do so, but most stick around awhile and enjoy the fellowship.

The second portion of this question concerns the length of time the group will remain together. Here again the options are plentiful. Most groups exist for a fixed amount of time whether it is a few weeks or several years. Groups with unstated time structures are not the best idea. A majority of people feel uncomfortable with, and consequently will not participate in, groups that lack clearly defined time parameters.

My preference is to meet as a group for one-year—actually

eleven months, taking the month of August off. This strategy translates into about forty-five to forty-eight sessions if holidays and other reasons for not meeting are factored in.

Given the various goals and objectives pursued by different groups, longer or shorter lengths of times may be appropriate. A California church I'm familiar with uses small groups to assimilate new members. These initial groups meet for only six weeks. At the end of that time, the participants are invited to join a more traditional group.

In general, I feel strongly that if a group—especially a process-oriented group—is to succeed it must meet for no less than one-and-a-half hours each week for a minimum of one year. But this is an ideal. Content- or task-oriented groups often meet for only the length of time it takes to cover the content or complete the task. Need-oriented groups are often ongoing, with membership changing on a regular basis.

What Do You Do When You Meet?

The question of what you should do when you meet is harder to answer than it may appear. The options are vast. To give order and purpose to the options, some small group advocates suggest a structural framework or categories of needed group activity. For example, the authors of *Good Things Come in Small Groups* (InterVarsity Press, 1985) recommend a four-fold structure: nurture, worship, community, and mission. Each of the four elements is seen as an important aspect of the group and needs some level of emphasis within every group meeting. Specific group activities are planned around this structure.

In my way of thinking, any individual group cannot do or be all things. It needs to be a part of an overall philosophy of ministry that includes different activities or programs designed to contribute to the various dimensions of making disciples. So, if some of these dimensions are better facilitated within other programs or types of groups, I see no need to make them a *regular* part of every group's format. Small groups must focus on those dimensions that are best facilitated in a group context and are not being addressed in other settings.

At this point allow me to make a subtle but important distinction. It is possible to differentiate between the group's stated agenda—reflected in the type or the main activity or reason for meeting—and the underlying dynamics that make a group successful. However, sometimes the dynamics become the group's main activity, the reason the group exists. In process-oriented groups, for example, group dynamics, group building, or process becomes the central concern. What the group *does* when gathered together is secondary to what the group (and individual members) *become* as a result of the meetings.

As you decide what to do when you meet, keep in mind the general goals discussed in chapter 1, your group's type (i.e., process, content, task, or need), and your group's specific objectives. One or more of the following activities may be appropriate for your meetings:

- ◆ Bible study (by book or topic)
- ◆ Discussion (topic, sermons, issue)
- ◆ Bible study workbooks
- ◆ Prayer
- ◆ Sharing of personal joys, prayer requests, needs, and so on
- ◆ Singing hymns and choruses
- ◆ Silent prayer and meditation on God
- ◆ Evangelistic Bible study
- ◆ Casual fun (often called "fellowship")
- ◆ Defined task (choir, visitation, leadership board)
- ◆ Bible memorization

More alternatives and many combinations are possible, only your imagination limits you. Three things can have an influence on your choices. First, you may find it preferable to include more than one activity within any given group meeting. Second, and my favorite option, rotate the activities. My group includes personal sharing and prayer as part of every meeting, but rotates between sermon discussion, focused prayer, and casual fun as the primary group activities. This type of rotation has kept the group fresh and dynamic. And third, if your group is part of a larger groups' ministry that stipulates your group's format and activities, you don't need to concern yourself with other options. Just work hard to implement the stated format.

What Are You Going to Do with the Children?
I often hear the parents of young children express their frustration because they want to be in a group but can't find suitable child care.

Can you think of any creative alternatives to this situation? Here are some I have seen or used.

Have the children attend a church-sponsored program designed especially for them if there is one available. Parents are then able to attend their own meetings knowing that their children are well cared for. Scheduling is an essential part of this option. Adequate time must be allowed for parents to bring their children, travel to their group meeting, attend the meeting, and then return to pick up their children afterward.

My favorite option is to trade off with another group or individual. For example, I watch your kids on Tuesday night while you attend your group, then you watch mine on Wednesday evening while I go to my group.

Or, if you meet in a home that has a separate large room, one member of the group cares for the children, on a rotating basis.

If it is a workable option, hire one or more sitters to care for the children in a home separate from the one where the group meetings are held.

Another idea is to include the children—have a group made up of family units. This can work, but be alert to the fact that having children in the group significantly changes the role and potential benefit experienced by the adults.

Each of the above mentioned options has its pros and cons. So, before selecting one, don't forget to carefully analyze your specific situation to determine which option(s) best meets the members' needs.

KNOW YOUR GROUP MEMBERS

Every group is a collection of individuals. Each person brings to the group a set of experiences, opinions, ideas, attitudes, and expectations. The larger the group, the greater the number of these variables the leader must deal with. Success in knowing your group is directly related to the size of your group.

What Size Should Your Group Be?
The consensus opinion among small group experts places group size somewhere between two and fifteen people. My experience leads me

to suggest that twelve is the ideal group size. There is no magic in this number, but it is the figure Jesus Christ selected for His designated inner group—the disciples.

Think about it. If you increase a group's size beyond twelve members, you're expanding the number of potential relationships within the group that must be formulated and maintained. As group size increases, the complexity of interpersonal relationships expands geometrically. A group of twelve members has the potential for sixty-six different relationship combinations. Increasing the group size by just three persons, to fifteen, results in 105 possible relationships.

The larger a group grows, the more easily a member can hide. I don't mean hide in a physical sense, but in a spiritual, social, or emotional sense. A recent group I led started out with nine members. After several months the group was really starting to take shape, the relationships were solidifying. But because our church was growing and we wanted to assimilate new members, we discussed the options and decided to add eight more people. The dynamics of a nine-member group radically changed when it became a seventeen-member group. It was much easier for the quiet member to remain silent, the verbal member to dominate, the less-committed members to find excuses for not attending, and the fringe member to remain on the periphery. Of course these liabilities can be addressed. My point is that large groups can present major roadblocks, hindering you and your group members from getting to know one another.

In short, limiting your group's size to around twelve people is one of the best ways to avoid many obstacles and ensure the probability of having a successful group. But twelve is only an ideal. Larger groups can work if you are careful to put in an extra amount of time facilitating the group's communication and relationships.

How Was Your Group Formed?

Realizing how your group was formed is another important piece of information in knowing and serving your group. There are many ways for a group to become a group. However, the method is usually some variation of one of three general options: choice, specific assignment, or random assignment.

Allowing people to participate in the group of their choice is my preferred method of forming groups. It generates an "I want to be in this group" attitude from the very beginning, because adults prefer making their own choices. The best application of this method is to post the group leaders, formats, times, and locations, and then ask interested persons to select the group that best fits their schedule and/or preferences. When a group reaches twelve members it is closed. New groups can be offered at stated times throughout the year. Some form of "choice" method in forming groups has merit because it provides options and the implementation specifics are readily adaptable to most situations.

Many churches and organizations assign people to groups. This strategy permits a more precise management of group size and function. One large church I'm familiar with interviews each person and then assigns that person to a group. Careful attention is given to having the right mix of individuals within each group. New groups are begun as needed. This is a good method when high control within a groups' ministry is desired. Yet, it can appear heavy handed and lacks the element of choice most adults prefer.

The last option is forming groups by some means of random assignment. Persons who want to be in a group write basic information (name, address, telephone number) on a short form and place it in some type of receptacle. The total number of participants is divided by ten or twelve to determine the number of groups needed. Next, names are randomly drawn and assigned to a group until all the groups are filled. This option works well in situations where the people already know each other and are open to being in any group, such as in adult classes. It can be a workable strategy, but I've never seen it used to form groups within an entire church.

Regardless of the specific method used to form your groups, it is wise to make sure the people involved feel comfortable with the procedure. This fact is especially true in smaller churches.

Are Group Members Cross-Generational, or Close in Age?
The debate rages: Should groups be homogeneous (same age, social status, etc.) or heterogeneous (mixed ages, social status, etc.)? Good reasoning exists on both sides of the issue. Both approaches can work, but which is better? I prefer homogeneous groups in terms of age; other factors can be heterogeneous. My bias comes from

having experienced both approaches. People who are approximately the same age (a five- to ten-year spread) have more in common. This commonality promotes closer friendships and facilitates quicker group development. Of course, this assumes the purpose of the group is wider than merely a task orientation. The group exists to enable relationships and spiritual growth.

Given this assumption, groups that include members of mixed age groups are workable, but normally the groups take longer to develop, experience reduced levels of communication, and struggle with the wider diversity of needs represented among the members. Nevertheless, many churches elect to structure their entire groups' ministry around cross-generational groups. The benefits associated with such a grouping strategy are considered more important than any potential liabilities. Cross-generational groups are especially common in small churches where the numbers of people within the various age groups are not sufficient to warrant age-graded groups.

Is Your Group Open or Closed?

Some groups have a fixed or stable membership, while others are designed to accept members at any time. Both approaches have strengths and weaknesses. Closed groups are better for developing long-term intimate relationships, but can become exclusive. Open groups work well in quickly assimilating people, but often don't provide the stable relationships conducive to intimate sharing and caring.

Groups that are primarily content-oriented, such as Bible studies, lend themselves to an "all come" approach. On the other hand, groups that stress relationships and are primarily process-oriented need to have fixed memberships. Jesus' group, the apostles, was a closed group. One good exception to the closed group principle is the support or recovery group, which is designed to focus on a unique need or issue, such as divorce, addiction, grief/loss, singles, aging parents, and so on. In these situations an open, cross-generational group strategy is often preferred.

A church or organization need not limit itself to only one type of group. With careful planning, it may be desirable to have some groups that are open and others that are closed. Likewise, going back to an earlier issue, some groups may be age-graded while others are cross-generational. The larger a church grows, the more it becomes necessary to provide a diversity within its groups' ministries.

What Motivates People to Participate in Your Group?

An important aspect of knowing your group is understanding why the members are in the group, what motivates their participation. Knowing this information is not only useful, it's necessary. The success of your group is directly related to the members' motives for being there. As is the case with most small group issues, a wide assortment of reasons is possible. Chapter 3 included a list of principles with interesting facts about people's motivation for joining and participating in small groups. Some of the reasons are a bit disturbing. Yet, people are people. We don't always do what we do for the right reasons.

Clarifying the members' motivations and expectations early in the life of your group saves you from countless aggravations. If your group is just starting, take time to discuss these matters. If your group is already down the road, and you haven't clarified these issues, stop now and do it. This advice is based on the knowledge that if you don't, you face a potential rocky road or even a major disaster until you do.

How Do You Get to Know Your Group Members?

After a period of time you'll start to make generalizations about how the members of your group act and feel as an unit. You'll begin talking about the group as if it were an individual: "My group does this" or "my group feels this way." This language pattern is a good sign that the group is beginning to solidify. However, it's important not to lose sight of the fact that a group is a collection of human beings. As such, individual members must always be an important focus of your leadership. You must be careful to get to know and build relationships with each member, avoiding the tendency to treat the members as if they were transparent and lacked attitudes and opinions apart from the group.

From the very beginning *both* individual and group identities must be emphasized. A significant portion of the time spent during the first meetings should be devoted to getting to know and appreciate one another. The benefits are twofold: allowing people to get to know one another, while at the same time laying a solid foundation for group unity. Many methods are available to accomplish this requirement, but the methods aren't as important as actually doing it. An early emphasis on relationships is especially essential for process- or need-oriented groups, but relationships are of secondary concern for content- or task-oriented groups.

Ongoing efforts within and outside the scheduled group meetings are essential. It is profitable to periodically set aside time during a meeting to evaluate your group processes and relationships. Chapter 7 can be of assistance to you in planning this agenda item. And as time permits, anything you are able to do outside the group meetings—such as having a few members over for dinner, telephone calls, short notes, personal meetings over coffee—greatly enhances the growth and development of the members of your group, and the group itself.

SITUATION CHECKLIST

The following checklist may help you clarify the conditions under which your group exists. In completing the checklist you'll gain an accurate picture of the dynamics affecting your group. Before starting, you may find it profitable to go back and review chapters 1 through 4 to refresh your memory.

Your Small Group Situation

Instructions: In a separate journal or notebook, record the most appropriate answer or provide a written response for each of the following items. There are no right or wrong answers. The object of this activity is to assist you in identifying the characteristics or conditions under which your group exists.

Biblical Foundations
1. Speaking for myself, I am . . .
   ____ fully convinced of the biblical priority for small groups.
   ____ mostly convinced of the biblical priority for small groups.
   ____ slightly convinced of the biblical priority for small groups.
   ____ not convinced there is a biblical priority for small groups.

2. For the most part I think my church leadership is . . . (Choose one of the responses under question 1.)

3. For the most part I think my senior pastor is . . . (Choose one of the responses under question 1.)

Your Leadership Profile
4. On a scale of one to five, rate yourself as to what best represents your present status for each of the following qualifications (with 1 representing a definite no, and 5 representing a definite yes):

   a. I am a seasoned Christian.
   b. I have a growing relationship with Christ.
   c. I am committed to caring for people.
   d. I have a desire to serve.
   e. I have a willingness to learn.
   f. I have resolved to spend the necessary time.

5. My role as a small group leader . . .
   ___ is outlined in a written job description.
   ___ is a matter of well-defined oral tradition.
   ___ lacks a written job description.
   ___ is self-defined.
   ___ Other (please specify).

6. Think about the characteristics of a *servant-leader*. On a scale of one to ten, with ten being the ideal servant-leader, how close do you come to this ideal?

7. Reflect on the nature and demands of *situational leadership*. Using a scale of one to ten, with ten being the highest, rate your level of understanding of this concept.

8. Review the *functional behaviors* that promote shared leadership. Which one do you most need to work on?

The Status of Your Group's Development
9. How long has your group been meeting? Or, when will it begin meeting?

10. To the best of your knowledge and understanding of the five phases of group development, which phase would you say your group is in?

11. Are you using a written group covenant? If you are not, write down the reason(s) for not doing so.

The Characteristics of Your Group

12. Based on the primary focus or central reason why your group exists, would you classify it as a process-, content-, task-, or need-oriented group, or something other than one of these (please specify)?

13. Beyond the general goals that all groups should pursue, what specific goals and objectives is your group attempting to accomplish?

14. Which of the following statements applies to how your group fits into the life of your church? (More than one may apply.)
    ___ My group is part of a larger groups' ministry sponsored by the church.
    ___ My group is not part of an organized groups' ministry within my church.
    ___ My group is part of a larger groups' ministry sponsored by an organization other than my local church.
    ___ My group is not connected with a local church or another organization.
    ___ Group membership is expected of all adult members in my church or organization.
    ___ Groups membership is an option for adult members.
    ___ Groups are stressed and given high visibility.
    ___ Groups aren't stressed or given any special attention.

15. Record the details of your group meetings, including day, time, place, length of each meeting, and total length of time the group will remain together.

16. The format of our group, what we do when we meet, is . . .
    ___ required of all groups in our church.
    ___ is flexible and changes from week to week.

___ includes (name all activities), which are rotated from week to week.

___ is fixed; we (name all activities).

___ is in the process of being decided.

___ Other (please specify).

17. Does your group care for members' children? If so, write down your method.

18. How many members are there in your group? Of this number, approximately how many attend each meeting?

19. Record two things you have done, or are planning to do, to personally get to know each group member.

20. How was your group formed? Were the members assigned to the group or did they choose to be members, or was another method used? (Please specify.)

21. Would you describe your group as being cross-generational (a mix of ages) or approximately the same age (five- to ten-year spread)?

22. When it comes to inviting or taking in new members, my group is . . .

___ open to all comers at any time.

___ "closed" after the first few weeks.

___ undefined.

___ Other (please specify).

CHAPTER FIVE

Leading
Your Group

I n accepting the role of a small group leader you undertook the responsibility to facilitate your group's successful growth and development. Inherent in this enabling role are various tasks or functions. Seven of the most common tasks are discussed in this chapter: planning meetings, decision making, worship, discussion, sharing, Bible study, prayer, and selecting resources. We'll briefly examine each one.

PLANNING A GROUP MEETING

Every group, including yours, presents a distinctive set of characteristics and requirements. Given this diversity, coming up with a generic strategy for planning group meetings is tough. Nevertheless, based on my own experience, I've come up with the following procedures. Feel free to tailor them to fit your situation.

Step One: Prayer—The first (and continuing) step is prayer. This vital activity keeps you plugged in to our divine Power Source. If you're like me, it's far too easy to start out on your own and neglect this first requirement.

Pray that God would give you wisdom and understanding. Pray for insight as you plan. Pray for each member of the group. Pray that the group meeting would bring honor to Christ. Pray earnestly! When it comes to planning for and leading your group—and all the other things you do as well—too much prayer is impossible.

Step Two: Content—The specifics of your meeting depend on your group's format. Different formats require the preparation of different "content." The most obvious example is Bible study. You'll need to analyze the passage to determine its meaning and application, identify the main points you want to cover with the group, and gather any supporting information you may wish to use. Support information may include discussion questions or devised case studies. If planning for a task-oriented group, it might be appropriate to outline the specific things you want to accomplish, collect any useful background information, and identify any guidelines that must be followed. Depending on the type of group, the content you prepare forms the basis for your next step.

Step Three: Process—Knowing what you want to cover or accomplish, now you must turn your attention to the details of structuring the actual events of the meeting. Specifically, what you're going to do, what you want the group members to do, and the time sequencing for both. The object is to outline the activities for the specific group meeting in question. If your group follows a set format of activities each week your job is simplified. My group rotates its format so I must make process decisions on a weekly basis.

This step is often undertaken simultaneously with the previous step. But when structuring the process, keep in mind you are putting together the ideal plan or course of action. Flexibility is important. Should the need become apparent, be ready to abandon your planned process. This is possible only if you are prepared with a plan to set aside if and when good reasons present themselves.

Step Four: Details—Having prepared your content and decided on the appropriate process, now you need to identify and arrange for any details. I am referring to those particulars that may have been identified in steps two and three. Now is the time to literally gather any materials you may need, ask a member to do something, make sure everyone knows that the time has been changed, and so on. Attention to small details makes for a large success!

Step Five: Follow-up—The final step in preparing for your group meeting entails reviewing previous meetings to determine if your planning up to this point is sufficient. If you asked your group members to come to the next meeting ready to share something, but you haven't included that activity in your meeting plan, now is the time to make the adjustment. On a different front, you may have said that you would do something or contact somebody. Do it! Follow-up may also include any reporting that is necessary if your group is a part of a larger groups' ministry. Many churches ask their group leaders to file weekly reports. In conclusion, this is your final catch-all step, your last chance to plan for, recall, pick up, or secure something prior to the meeting.

I want to stress long-range planning. Careful planning for your group's next meeting is very important, but it isn't sufficient. Your group is best served if you work together and plan further in advance.

My group has found it helpful to use a three-month planning calendar tailored to our specific needs (see page 84). It is structured around our Wednesday evening meetings. It includes places for listing weekend activities. During the last month appearing on our current calendar, we plan and fill out a calendar for the next three-month period. Normally, this takes only the first few minutes of a regular meeting. When completed it serves as a handy reminder of group (and possibly other church) activities.

You may choose to include several types of information on your calendar. Of course, you'll want to note the specifics for each meeting—what will be done and who is in charge. If you meet in different locations, be sure to mark that. Important dates like birthdays and holidays can be included. Be creative. The planning calendar can become an important tool in facilitating the success of your group.

If your group is part of a ministry sponsored by your church, you may be required to follow some type of centrally prepared calendar. In addition, certain weekly or monthly reporting forms are frequently expected. Find out if any such requirements exist. If they do, be sure to complete them in a timely and adequate manner. Paperwork is a normal part of leadership. While it may not be exciting, it is important.

DECISION MAKING

Assorted decisions will face you and the members of your group at various points in your group's life. These decisions may encompass large issues, such as the nature and format of the group, or be limited to minor administrative details. Regardless of the magnitude of each decision, your leadership in the decision-making process is crucial.

CARINGROUP THREE-MONTH CALENDAR

October

Wednesday	Friday	Saturday
4	6	7
11	13	14
18	20	21
25	27	28

November

Wednesday	Friday	Saturday
1	3	4
8	10	11
15	17	18
22	24	25
29		

December

Wednesday	Friday	Saturday
	1	2
6	8	9
13	15	16
20	22	23
27	29	30

Before going on, it's a good idea to distinguish between *decision making* and *problem solving*. Decision making is the process of choosing between two or more alternatives. Problem solving, on the other hand, is a more comprehensive procedure intended to help a person or group resolve an unsatisfactory set of circumstances. It incorporates decision making, but decision making is a more fundamental activity that isn't always problem centered. Hence, our present focus is on decision making. The larger topic of problem solving is discussed in the next chapter.

Decision making deals with two questions: Who makes the decisions in a group? By what method does a group make decisions?

Who Makes the Decisions in a Group?

Given our discussion in chapter 2, you probably answered, "the whole group." Ideally, I agree. However, real life isn't always that simple. There may be a number of decisions made for you even prior to the group's first meeting, for example, the purpose and format of the group, how long the group meets, or where the group meets. The likelihood of such decisions being resolved outside of your group is greatest when you're part of an organized small groups' program. The need for clarity, consistency, and control may require all groups in the program to maintain uniform requirements. If this is the case, many decisions affecting your group will be made by those individuals who oversee the total program. Implementing the decision is your responsibility.

On the flip side, if your group is "independent"—not part of a larger well-organized program or only loosely associated with other groups in your church or organization—you'll have many decisions to make. It is very tempting, as the leader, to make the necessary decisions for the group. *Avoid this tendency at all costs!* Remember, the goal is shared leadership. If you make all the decisions this ideal is squelched.

Group decisions take longer to make than those made by one individual, but the results frequently are far superior. The old adage "two heads are better than one" is true. You may disagree—especially if you're the "strong leader" type—but my experience has convinced me the adage is right. I'm willing to invest the time in group decision making if a stronger, mutually derived, supported decision is the result. To be honest, this ideal isn't always the way it turns out. Nevertheless, making decisions in the group is definitely worth the effort!

By What Methods Does a Group Make Decisions?

While other strategies do exist, decisions made by consensus, majority vote, or designated person(s) are the most popular options selected by small groups. No method is perfect, each has its strengths and weaknesses. Yet, they all tend to promote a sense of participation and ownership among the group members, especially if the members are allowed to select the method of decision making.

Regardless of the method, some prerequisites are important. Certain attitudes and standards must precede and guide the process.

Prior Attitudes

Share responsibility for the decision—Group members must "own" the decision. This is critical. If the members aren't ardent supporters, the decision is little more than useless. The decision-making method as well as the actual decision must have the total support of the group.

Seek the best results—Take the high road and pursue the best decision possible. Quality decisions are products of careful analysis and consideration. The best decision will yield the maximum benefit for the individual members and the group as a whole.

Seek to discern God's will—This standard is the most important, but it is so obvious it's easily overlooked. We often presume upon it and lose it in the shuffle. Remember, discovering God's will is the heart of decision making in your group. Always keep in mind the question, "What would God have us do?"

Methods

Consensus—Consensus is my preferred method for group decision making. It's not the easiest way to make decisions, but it produces the best results. I define consensus as a *tentative working agreement.* This means the group members agree to go with the alternative every member can "live with" and support. Not that everyone completely agrees, but that they are willing to tentatively accept the course of action.

Voting—Making a decision by a show of hands, saying aye, or using some form of written response—voting is probably the procedure most often used in our churches. Voting is very much in keeping with the democratic mindset in the United States. Consequently, voting is also the most common decision-making procedure used in small groups. Nevertheless, it is a method with problems. Can God's will be discerned through a majority vote?

Designated person—The group members may choose to designate someone—perhaps the leader or someone else—to make the decision on their behalf. This person (may be more than one) is asked to explore the alternatives, make a decision, and report back to the group. Often this is a good alternative when the decision has a low effect on the group.

Four steps are essential to good decision making, regardless of the method used to make the final decision.

Essential Steps

Clearly define your needed decision—This step helps the group avoid wasted time and energy. Failure to do so may lead to a decision that doesn't resolve the issue. Groups that clearly understand the situation that calls for a choice make better decisions.

Carefully establish your criteria—Identify and rank the standards the decision must meet. Criteria are conditions or requirements by which alternatives can be evaluated. The goal is to identify—as well as possible—the necessary criteria that if followed will yield the highest results.

Evaluate your options—Using the established criteria, look closely at your options on the basis of positive and negative consequences. After listing all workable options, evaluate each in light of its consequences. Effective groups are able to anticipate all negative ramifications, and thereby eliminate the worst options, while identifying the optimum choice.

Select one tentative option—This alternative represents the best choice given the circumstances—a selection that best serves the immediate and long-term needs of the group. It is held loosely and acted on until the situation dictates reevaluation.

You may find these hints helpful in assisting your group to make quality decisions:

◆ Allow adequate time. Rushed decisions are risky and rarely the best decisions.

◆ State your opinions convincingly, after all you're a member of the group. Avoid demanding your own way.

◆ Accept stalemate if it occurs. Find the next best alternative acceptable to all.

◆ Seek out different opinions. They are useful in selecting alternatives and evaluating possible outcomes.

◆ Assure that a decision is supported by the entire group before it is implemented. Avoid win-lose situations.

◆ Stay flexible. Decisions can be changed if the need arises and the group is agreeable.

WORSHIP

Worship is a vital part of many small group meetings. It helps set the tone for the meeting by assisting your group members to clear their minds of the daily grind and instead focus on God. Worship may serve as the focal activity for the entire meeting, though most groups worship during the opening five to ten minutes.

According to the *Evangelical Dictionary of Theology* (Zondervan Corporation, 1984), the word *worship* within the context of the New Testament church means "to ascribe to Him [God] the worth of which He is worthy." My good friends Ron Allen and Gordon Borror pick up on this idea in their book, *Worship: Rediscovering the Missing Jewel* (Multnomah Press, 1982). They define worship as "an active response to God whereby we declare His worth." To me this means praising God by focusing on His nature, actions, and words.

Allen and Borror suggest the essence of worship is the *celebration* of God: "When we worship God, we celebrate Him: We extol Him, we sound His praises, we boast in Him." In doing this they warn that worship isn't primarily a state of art, but a state of heart. I like this idea. Worship isn't what we do as much as it is the attitude behind what we do.

Worship is capable of taking on different forms within your group. It may include reading Scripture, meditation, singing, verbal praise, silence, written statements, or even shouting and dancing. The last suggestions may not be appropriate in your situation, but they are biblical concepts of worship (2 Samuel 6:14-15).

What about the posture of worship? Often we limit it to an expression of our mouths—what we say or sing. But our entire bodies can be instruments of worship. Bowing our heads, lifting up our hands in praise, kneeling, or even prostrating ourselves are all pictured in Scripture.

The following are a few practical guidelines to assist you in leading worship in your group.

Plan—Like the other elements of the group meeting, be sure to carefully plan the worship activities. Stifling or legislating spontaneity isn't the idea. You merely want to assist the group by providing helpful worship formats and materials.

Model—As with other group activities, you as the leader set the tone. Your genuine worshipful attitude and practices must be contagious.

Enlist—There may be one or two members of your group who would like to plan and lead the worship within your group. You don't necessarily need to serve as the worship leader all the time.

Creative—Remember, worship may take more than one form. Use your imagination. Avoid doing one thing, such as singing, every time you approach worship.

Comfortable—Different groups feel comfortable doing different things. If your members initially feel uncomfortable raising their hands, praying out loud, singing, or whatever, go slow. Encourage participation without forcing anyone.

Context—Worship is influenced by our surroundings. You don't need stained glass windows and wooden pews, but pay attention to your context. Shut a door, close or open a drape, arrange the chairs, and so on, to make your setting conducive to worship.

Content—Your group may want to take time to study the biblical idea and practice of worship. Make sure you practice what you study. Avoid allowing it to become merely an exercise of the mind.

DISCUSSION

Discussion is the procedural glue that holds most groups together. It is the primary method by which we exchange ideas, opinions, and feelings. It serves as a path for making group decisions and facilitating interpersonal sharing. Consequently, leading a discussion is one of the most important skills small group leaders must cultivate.

In leading discussions you perform several critical roles. Four are identified by Stewart and Fishwick (*Group Talk,* 1986). As a *catalyst* you cause people to think individually and then to interact with each other. As a *guide* (I prefer the word *enabler*), you keep the discussion on track while facilitating participation. As a *clarifier* your task is to clarify questions and comments so that each person has the maximum opportunity to understand and apply what is being said. And as an *affirmer,* you encourage others by recognizing the value in every person and each contribution.

On the opposite side, here are some behaviors that you must avoid. Abstain from becoming the *answer person* with the tendency to answer every question or comment. Refuse serving as the *last word,* the final authority or opinion on a point of discussion. Refrain from becoming the *monopolizer,* the person who does all the talking.

Questions are your primary tool in planning and leading good discussions. Effective questions get the discussion rolling, explore the topic or biblical passage, and draw out the application to our individual and corporate lives.

Writing and asking good questions is a real art. They must be *clear, relevant,* and *stimulating.* If no one understands what you're asking, the question is ambiguous and lacks clarity. A question is relevant if it fits the topic and needs an answer. "So what?" or a big yawn are typical responses to unstimulating questions.

Three distinct types of questions can serve the group's discussion. I've seen at least five or six different names for the three types, but the various names all reflect the same meanings:

- ◆ Launching questions
- ◆ Understanding questions
- ◆ Applying questions

Launching Questions
The objective of launching questions is to get the discussion rolling. Launching questions pose a dilemma, ask an opinion, or seek information. Everyone in the group should be able to give an answer.

Within Bible study, launching questions often take the form of information questions. They invite the participants to discuss the who, what, when, and where contained in the passage. The answer to a launching or information question should be at hand, in the text, from the person's experience, or legitimately open to speculation. Here are some examples:

◆ Why does man want to deny God's existence?
◆ What are the seven reasons stated in the passage?
◆ How does the author describe the situation?

Understanding Questions

Called exploration or discovery questions by some authors, the purpose of understanding questions is to draw principles out of the Scripture passage being studied, the topic under discussion, or the facts being considered. In Bible studies, understanding questions are used to help participants comprehend the author's meaning. (One word of caution: Avoid going around the circle and asking each person, "What do you think this means?" This and other similar techniques merely "pool the ignorance" and potentially violate the standards of proper biblical interpretation.) In general discussions, understanding questions help the group go beyond initial observations and facilitate a deeper sensitivity to the issues. Here are a few examples:

◆ What is Paul's meaning in Ephesians 2:12 when he says, "Work out your salvation with fear and trembling"?
◆ Why should a Christian pray?
◆ When you said you didn't care what happened, what did you mean?

Applying Questions

Application questions help the members apply the facts and principles to their own lives, both individually and corporately. The idea of corporate application is important. Often we limit application to an individual response. But as members of the Body of Christ, applying questions must also explore relevant corporate applications.

This means that the questions, "What must *I* do in response?" and "How should *we* respond?" are both necessary. These are examples of applying questions:

◆ What can we do as a group this week to demonstrate the love of God?
◆ What is one way you can improve your prayer life?
◆ How can you become a caring person, even when you don't feel like it?

So, we have determined that questions must be clear, relevant, and stimulating. We have also identified three types of questions: launching, understanding, and applying. Given these positive standards, here are five "technical" flaws you need to avoid when formulating your questions.

Problems to Avoid
First, avoid questions that can be answered yes or no. It doesn't leave room for discussion if the logical response to your question is a simple yes or no. This type of flawed question is the new leader's most common mistake.

Second, avoid long, wordy questions. Brief, short questions work best. They require fewer mental gymnastics to remember and then answer.

Third, avoid using double negatives. Doesn't it make sense not to write questions that use enigmatic words? Did you catch the point?

Fourth, avoid putting questions within a question. Compound questions need to be broken down into singular, uncomplicated questions. For instance, three separate questions would be better than, "Which characteristic of the fruit of the Spirit do you think Christians have the greatest difficulty expressing, and why is it they have such difficulty, or how can they overcome their fear of expression?"

Fifth, avoid either-or questions. Asking an either-or question limits the answer to a choice between two options. It forces the group members to select an answer they may not have given or would prefer to explain. A useful example of this flaw is found in the question, "Why must a Christian be either a Baptist or a Presbyterian?"

Do you remember all that? Let's have a little fun and find out what you remember. Take the following quiz to test your knowledge on writing effective questions. When you're finished, the last page of this chapter gives some possible answers you can use to check your responses.

Good Questions Quiz

Instructions: Each of the following six questions, based on James 1:2-4, violates one or more of the principles of good questions. Use these three considerations to evaluate each question: (1) determine if it's a launching, understanding, or applying question; (2) decide if it's clear, relevant, and stimulating; and (3) identify any flaws you can detect. (You may want to review pages 90-92.)

1. What are some ways we can "consider it all joy" when we encounter trials, and how is it possible to develop endurance?
2. Why is it not acceptable to not define *endurance* as being either tough skinned or long suffering?
3. Are there seven key words contained in these three verses?
4. Since the eloquent book of James magnificently renders an exquisite portrayal of our culpability for appropriate mental states when encountering tribulations, what are the vicissitudes relevant to a comprehension of the concept *various* in the essayist's delineation of trials?
5. In what ways is it not possible for you to avoid knowing you aren't likely to cry when faced with testing?
6. As we get started tonight, I'm interested in knowing if you want to lack for nothing and why people seem to fall apart or ignore difficulties in their lives, plus why we can consider it joy when faced with these difficulties.

Useful Suggestions for Leading Discussions
Plan ahead. Write out your questions before the discussion. Avoid asking questions off the top of your head. Too often impromptu questions lack focus and clarity.

Focus on your task. When leading a discussion you must concentrate on your task: leading the discussion. It is easy to get caught up in the conversation and forget your leadership responsibilities.

Start slowly. Begin with impersonal, nonthreatening questions and work toward asking personal questions. A common error new discussion leaders make is to jump right in and ask questions that the group members find highly threatening.

Silence is acceptable. Don't get nervous if no one answers your question immediately. Give the group members time to think. However, if everyone has a puzzled look on his or her face, you may need to restate the question or clarify your meaning.

Be sensitive. There will be differences among your group members. Not everyone is comfortable speaking up in group situations, my wife, for example. Forcing this type of person to join the discussion is counterproductive.

Be willing to help. For instance, you may need to help an overly verbal person control his or her participation. This usually means speaking with that person outside of the group.

Don't put people on the spot. Avoid calling on people by name in the early stages of your group (unless you already know your group members well). Balanced participation doesn't require compelling people to speak.

SHARING

Sharing is a form of discussion that permits us to open our lives to one another. It is an important part of being a small group member. I think the majority of believers want the privilege of sharing, but it makes many of us extremely nervous. Some degree of difficulty in sharing our lives with one another is common, especially for men. This fact is particularly true when the sharing is focused on our innermost thoughts and emotions.

Rarely do our American and Christian cultures provide us with natural opportunities to learn, practice, and value interpersonal and group communication skills. Occasionally, we are encouraged in these areas, but typically little other than the exhortation is offered. Your small group can help offset this dilemma.

Sharing may take place at many different points within the group meetings. It can precede prayer, be a part of discussions focusing on applicational issues, be prompted by life-related Bible study, or be a part of casual conversations before or after the meetings. It fits in almost anywhere when you realize there are different levels of sharing.

My experience with groups has helped me identify four distinct, but interrelated, levels of sharing.

Level one: Non-personal general information—This is the most casual form of sharing. I tell the group members common facts I know about other people, our church, or other situations with which I'm familiar. It's important information, but it isn't directly related to me or harmful to anyone else. Little or no personal risk is experienced by the person sharing at this level.

Level two: Non-personal related information—Circumstances shared are related to me, but not personally. Sharing is based on firsthand involvement with a situation. The association may be casual or extensive. Usually the information shared deals with everyday events in the lives of friends, relatives, or coworkers. Personal risk at this level is through the possibility of association.

Level three: Personal factual information—"Just the facts, please" was the frequent phrase used by Sergeant Joe Friday in the old television series *Dragnet.* This initial level of personal sharing consists of disclosing information that is factual, but not necessarily sensitive or potentially embarrassing. I merely divulge those pieces of factual data about myself that I feel comfortable telling—common descriptions, routine activities, plans, and events. It can be described as the "name, rank, and serial number" approach. But this type of sharing shouldn't be cold and mundane. You can ask for funny or interesting stories, nicknames, childhood adventures, favorite activities, or other similar types of personal factual information.

Level four: Personal intimate information—Present or past attitudes, inner feelings, behavior, emotions, and experiences are the focus of sharing at the intimate personal level. These are private and confidential issues. Embarrassment, or perhaps even guilt and shame, must be dealt with and overcome. Confession of sin is perhaps appropriate (James 5:16). A high degree of personal spiritual, social, and psychological risk is associated with this level of sharing.

The longer a group is together and is successful in advancing through the stages of group development, the easier it becomes for members to share at the advanced levels. However, some groups never progress to levels three and four. Their group's purpose or goals don't facilitate such sharing, or for whatever reason, they aren't successful in achieving the comfort level associated with the group maturity required to deal with intimate sharing.

As the group leader, you'll need to set the pace in assisting your group members to feel comfortable with sharing at all four levels. Here are some tips to help you:

+ *Set the example.* If you want your members to feel comfortable sharing, you must be willing to share first.
+ *Be patient.* Don't expect everyone from the very start to share at the fourth level. Start at the lower levels, working your way up to the higher levels.
+ *Stress honesty.* Don't avoid true feelings, emotions, and opinions.
+ *Practice acceptance.* Avoid acting shocked when someone shares startling information. Instead, communicate acceptance.
+ *Accept differences.* Different people have different levels of comfort when it comes to speaking in a group setting. Not everyone is as verbal as you'd like.
+ *Avoid pushing.* Some members are quiet by nature. Forcing them to share isn't a good idea. Allow them to wait until they're ready.

BIBLE STUDY

Bible study is the most common format used in small groups, especially within evangelical churches. In fact, many people equate Bible study and small groups. While this is not necessarily true, Bible study is one of the best format options your group can choose.

An excellent resource you may want to purchase and use is Richard Warren's *12 Dynamic Bible Study Methods for Individuals and Groups* (Victor Books, 1981). The book is packed full of super methods for making Bible study interesting and productive.

You can find the specifics of various Bible study methods in other resources such as Warren's book. Here are a few basic suggestions you'll want to keep in mind in order to lead successful group Bible studies.

All Bible study sessions contain four basic steps: (1) approach the Word, (2) explore the Word, (3) discover the Word, and (4) apply the Word. In approaching the Word the idea is to arouse the members' interest and curiosity to study the passage under consideration. Exploring the Word involves discerning what the passage says—its context and content. Identifying the meaning of the passage and its principles, facts, commands, and promises is achieved in discovering the Word. And the last step, applying the Word, is aimed at helping the group members apply the biblical truth to their individual and corporate lives.

The ultimate goal of Bible study is application. God wants us to act on the Word, not just know its facts. Therefore, never be satisfied with just interpreting the passage. While interpretation is very important, it must not be viewed as the sole reason for studying God's Word. James 1:22 tells us to be "doers of the word."

The best group Bible studies are discussions, not lectures. Each member should have the opportunity to discuss and interact with the other group members. Your role as the leader is to facilitate the active participation of the members, not dominate the discussion or give the answers.

The good Bible study leader knows how to ask excellent questions. Questions can stimulate the members' desire to study the Word, facilitate the interpretation of the passage, and incite active application of the biblical truth. You may want to refer to the previous section that dealt with formulating and asking questions.

Consider using a basic Bible study strategy based on these three questions:

◆ What does it say?
◆ What does it mean?
◆ How does it apply (to me and to us)?

Each group member should have his or her own copy of the Bible. Sharing a copy can work, but it puts limits on the active participation of members who do so.

Provide Bible study resources. It is very useful to have resources on hand, such as a concordance, a Bible dictionary, a Bible handbook, a Bible atlas, and commentaries.

Use variety. Avoid the risk of boredom by using a variety

of Bible study methods. Nothing is worse than doing exactly the same thing week in and week out. Change the order of activities, the method of discussion, the leadership role, and so on.

I suggest you avoid "reading around the circle," having each person in turn read one or more Scripture verses. Why? First, people have the tendency not to listen to what's being read, but to silently practice reading their verses. Second, some adults have difficulty reading aloud, and you don't want to embarrass them. Instead, you may want to ask for a volunteer to read the passage.

Be realistic about how much you can discuss in one session. Having the goal of completing one chapter each session is okay, unless it interferes with the members' participation and restricts the opportunity for application. In my opinion it's better to cover three verses in depth, including application, than to force yourself to accomplish a specific goal and get through a certain amount of content.

Consider using a Bible study guide. There are many useful guides on the market. Your local Christian bookstore can help you locate the best one. Using a guide can be of great assistance. If you do this, make sure each member (or couple) has a copy.

I recommend not assigning homework, unless everyone has agreed beforehand. Expecting your members to study outside group meetings—especially if it requires a large amount of time and effort—can have negative results. They want to complete the work, but if they didn't have time they may not come that week, or worse yet, they sometimes drop out all together.

Rotate leadership. If you have willing members, it's a great idea to share the responsibility for leading the Bible study. Doing so promotes leadership development and instills the fact that every member of the Body of Christ can handle the Word of God, if the appropriate amount of time and effort are invested.

Plan ahead. The best Bible studies are the ones where the leader is prepared. Both the content and the group process must be well thought out and ready.

PRAYER

Just as it is in your own spiritual life, prayer is an essential activity for healthy small groups, regardless of the type of group. Yet praying aloud in a group makes many people nervous. They fear sounding stupid, not knowing what to say, or making mistakes. This shouldn't be the case, but it is.

As the leader, your job is to help your group members have positive experiences in group prayer. They need to see that prayer within the group is a unique privilege and responsibility, a joy rather than a trial. Be patient. Some people take longer to be convinced.

Remind the group members that ritualism and religious sounding words and phrases aren't needed. Instead, they should concentrate on saying things they really mean, using their own words. Praying exactly what they think or feel requires honesty and openness with God. Concern for how they sound to the other members isn't important. What is important is communicating with God from the heart.

Prayer may take different routes in order to communicate the variety of thoughts you and your group want to express. Scripture teaches us that there at least five general focuses of prayer:

◆ *Praise* for who and what God is (Hebrews 13:15).
◆ *Thanksgiving* for what God has done and is doing (Ephesians 5:20).
◆ *Confession* of our sin (Proverbs 28:13).
◆ Prayer for *others* (James 5:16).
◆ Prayer for *personal* needs (James 1:5).

Each area listed above can serve as the focal point for an entire prayer session. At other times you may wish to include them all. Some leaders feel that praise and thanksgiving must be included in every prayer. Regardless of the specifics, we are instructed to pray (1 Thessalonians 5:17). Here are some ideas for using prayer in your group.

Keep a group prayer journal. Record prayer items and keep track of God's answers.

Divide into smaller groups to pray for one another. For example, if your group has twelve members, subdivide into groups of three or four to pray specifically for those in the smaller group.

Have prayer partners. Pair off so that two group members can pledge to pray for each other on a daily basis. Between group meetings, use the telephone to keep in contact.

Dedicate whole group sessions to prayer. Study it, talk about it, and do it.

Encourage spontaneous prayer, rather than in a sequence. Praying around the circle may sound like a good idea, and it may be if the people in your group know each other well. But praying in turn can put undue pressure on people. No one should be forced to pray.

Use both silent and audible prayer. At times you may want to ask people to pray silently to themselves, or use silent prayer as preliminary preparation to set the tone for audible group prayer.

Ask one or two members to volunteer to prepare ahead of time for leading the group in prayer.

Plan a five minute presentation on each of the five focuses of prayer mentioned previously. Give one presentation each week, and then have the group focus its prayer on that topic.

Write prayers. Whether in response to a passage being studied or as a separate activity, writing prayers and then reading them out loud is a meaningful experience for many groups.

Restrict the amount of time spent sharing prayer requests before actually praying. It is easy to spend so much time mentioning requests that there isn't enough time left to pray. Try praying for each item after it's shared. Another idea is to ask for certain people to pray for specific requests.

Try topical prayer. As you begin to pray, name a specific issue, need, or person, allowing members to pray for each item before naming the next one. The prayers may be silent or aloud.

Pray spontaneously when a need arises. Consider these two examples. During a time of sharing, an expressed concern may trigger prayer to lift that need up to God immediately. The glory of God revealed in a passage being studied may move you to stop and offer prayers of praise.

RESOURCES

Helping your group select and use resources is an important part of your job. There are many published resources available to assist you and your group in accomplishing the activities mentioned in this chapter. The biggest problem is selecting from among all the alternatives. To help you decide, here are three guidelines.

First, many published materials are generic in nature. That is, they are written for an average group. Specific doctrinal issues appropriate to your group may be totally lacking. Therefore, feel free to tailor anything you purchase to your own needs—add or subtract material, take two sessions to cover a section rather than one, or combine material from two or more sources. One caution: It's illegal to photocopy and distribute copyrighted materials.

Second, materials that are truly designed for groups include both content and suggested group process. Many studies on the market today weren't designed specifically for groups. Whether a group or an individual uses them makes no difference. So, my advice is to find materials that were specifically designed for group use. Fortunately, the quality and the quantity of studies for groups are increasing.

Third, published materials are only as good as the person using them. Study and planning are still required. Don't allow yourself to fall into the trap of mindlessly using study or discussion guides.

Here are some resources you may want to investigate on the topics briefly covered in this chapter.

Bible Study

Coleman, Lyman, ed. *Serendipity Bible for Groups* (NIV). Littleton, CO: Serendipity House, 1988.

Hestenes, Roberta. *Using the Bible in Groups.* Philadelphia: Westminster Press, 1983.

Warren, Richard. *Twelve Dynamic Bible Study Methods for Individuals or Groups.* Wheaton, IL: Victor Books, 1981.

Decision Making

Griffin, Em. *Getting Together: A Guide for Good Groups,* chapter 4, "Methods of Decision Making." Downers Grove, IL: InterVarsity Press, 1982.

Johnson, David W., and Johnson, Frank P. *Joining Together: Group Theory and Group Skills,* chapter 3, "Decision Making." Third edition. Englewood Cliffs, NJ: Prentice-Hall, 1987.

Discussion

Griffin, Em. *Getting Together: A Guide for Good Groups,* chapter 5, "Leading a Discussion." Downers Grove, IL: InterVarsity Press, 1982.

Stewart, Ed, and Fishwick, Nina. *Group Talk!* Ventura, CA: Regal Books, 1986.

Planning Meetings

Baker, Steve, et al. *Small Group Leaders' Handbook,* chapter 11, "How to Plan and Lead a Small Group." Downers Grove, IL: InterVarsity Press, 1982.

Mallison, John. *Growing Christians in Small Groups,* chapter 3, "Keys for Effective Small Groups." Homebush West, Australia: Anzea Publishers, 1989.

Prayer

Demaray, Donald E. *How Are You Praying?* Grand Rapids, MI: Francis Asbury Press, 1985.

Getz, Gene A. *Praying for One Another.* Wheaton, IL: Victor Books, 1982.

Sproul, R. C. *Effective Prayer.* Wheaton, IL: Tyndale House, 1984.

Sharing

Ortlund, Anne. *Discipling One Another,* chapter 15, "Ingredient Three: Sharing." Waco, TX: Word Books, 1979.

Worship

Barker, Steve, et al. *Good Things Come in Small Groups,* chapter 15, "Worship Resources." Downers Grove, IL: InterVarsity Press, 1985.

Erickson, Craig D. *Participating in Worship: History, Theory and Practice.* Atlanta, GA: John Knox Press, 1989.

Kendrick, Graham. *Learning to Worship as a Way of Life.* Minneapolis, MN: Bethany House Publishers, 1984.

GOOD QUESTIONS QUIZ: POSSIBLE ANSWERS

I suggest these evaluations of the questions on page 93. It's likely that you came up with different conclusions.

1. Applying question, compound question, unclear
2. Understanding question, either-or, double negative
3. Launching question, irrelevant, yes or no
4. Understanding question, unstimulating, unclear, long and wordy
5. Applying question, irrelevant, double negative
6. Launching question, unclear, either-or, compound, long

CHAPTER SIX

Handling Your Group's Difficulties

W ouldn't it be wonderful if life were trouble free! But we all know it isn't. Most assuredly, you will face difficulties—perhaps even one or two serious problems—in leading your small group. Being prepared to handle the problems by having a strategy is an important part of leading your group.

TYPICAL PROBLEMS

Good planning and preparation help to fend off many problems before they arise. But even the best planning cannot account for every difficult situation you'll encounter. Therefore, knowing what conflicts commonly arise in groups is useful in preparing an adequate response. In my experience, most of the conflicts or difficulties groups face fit into one of five general areas, most of which are people problems.

Expectations—You and the members of your group come together expecting certain things to happen and not happen. Most members bring with them ideas—however slight they may be—of what the purpose of the group is, what the group does, how they'll profit from being a member, and the demands the group will place on them. If there are twelve group members, you may discover twelve (or more!) different sets of expectations. The potential for conflict between these different expectations definitely exists.

Participation patterns—As unique persons, group members manifest various verbal and nonverbal behavior patterns. Quiet members may say little or nothing because they are intimidated by an aggressive, highly verbal member. One person may dominate group discussions. Another may make jokes out of everything. Then there is the "academic" member who questions everyone's statements from a philosophical perspective. These examples could go on and on. The patterns of how the group members participate or don't participate may lead to conflict.

Meeting formats—What will we do, or what are we supposed to be doing? "I think we should have a Bible study." "No, we should spend our time praying for one another." "Let's not meet this week, but go to the football game instead." "I don't care what they said we should do, I think we need to. . . ." Comments such as these reflect disagreement over the group's agenda.

Leadership skills—Some problems arise because you and I lack certain leadership skills and/or stumble in applying those we do have. We may come on too strong at the wrong point in the group's development, or not strong enough. Conflict between members may cause serious problems because the leader allows the problem to fester rather than dealing with it. A wide range of other conflicts can arise when the leader fails to lead.

Administrative details—"I thought *you* were going to do that!" "What time is the meeting?" "Whose house is the meeting at tonight?" These questions all reflect potential administrative problems, difficulties with the details.

A FOUR-STEP STRATEGY

Different group leaders handle problems in different ways. Some just ignore any difficulties and hope they'll go away. Others handle problems by sticking their head in the sand and denying a problem even exists. Eternal optimists, they refuse to acknowledge anything less than an ideal situation. Some leaders are quick to acknowledge problems and seek to resolve them in responsible ways. Still others, at the opposite extreme, see doom and despair at every turn in the bend.

Realistically speaking, it is likely that you will encounter at least one or two problems. Therefore, you need to have a plan to resolve them. I'm not, of course, advocating going out and looking for problems. I am suggesting the usefulness of a general strategy for problem solving ready to be applied quickly when the need arises.

A prerequisite to any problem-solving strategy is a right attitude. When faced with a problem your positive mental and emotional response is vital. Keep in mind and practice these words of the Apostle James:

> Consider it all joy, my brethren, when you encounter various trials, knowing that the testing of your faith produces endurance. And let endurance have its perfect result, that you may be perfect and complete, lacking in nothing. But if any of you lacks wisdom, let him ask of God, who gives to all men generously and without reproach, and it will be given to him. (James 1:2-5)

James's admonition isn't addressed to group leaders specifically, but his ideas certainly can be claimed by those of us who lead groups.

Let me quickly point out three specific ideas from these verses. First, what should be my initial response? James says "joy." A joy based on knowing God is in control of the situation, no matter how difficult it may seem. Second, the inevitable trials or problems associated with leading a group are important ingredients in our spiritual growth. Problems are one of the tools God uses in molding and shaping our lives. And third, we can ask for God's wisdom in handling the problems our groups face and it will be given to us. That is God's promise, we need to act on it!

An essential part of claiming God's promise is using the brain He has given us. God doesn't expect us to be mindless robots. In your role as a group leader, this means having a general strategy for dealing with problems if and when they occur. Here's a four-step approach you may find helpful.

Step One: Recognition—Words such as "I sense you are upset, Tom," or "We need to deal with this difference of opinion," signal that the person speaking has recognized a problem and is assisting the persons directly involved, as well as all the group members, to acknowledge the difficulty. Problems cannot be dealt with until they are recognized. Sweeping conflict under the carpet doesn't work.

Step Two: Personalization—The aim of the second step is to put people at ease, not place blame on someone. Conflict frequently raises people's temperatures. It is easy to lose control and attack personalities rather than the problem or disagreement. Help everyone understand that problem solving is natural and needed. The goal is to help the group profit from the experience.

Step Three: Clarification—Clarifying the exact nature of the problem and pursuing the potential solutions. Defining the problem can be quick, or quite complicated. At times the real problem isn't what you see, hear, or think it is. The real difficulty is beyond your ability to identify, address, and clarify without special assistance. But assuming that in most cases your assessment of the problem is correct, what are the acceptable alternatives?

Step Four: Resolution—The final step is to select the best alternative and put it into action.

Problem solving is easier said than done. Why? Because dealing with problems is dealing with people, and people don't always fit into nice four-step strategies. Nevertheless, with ample care and sensitivity this sequence of steps can serve you well.

In those extreme cases when a member is unwilling to cooperate with the group's attempts at problem solving, you'll need to deal with that person outside of the group. In a really rare case, you may find it necessary to ask the person to withdraw from the group. Take heart, in other instances, a friendly chat may be all that is needed.

Don't be shy in seeking outside help if you cannot solve the problem within the group. I suggest you contact your pastor or small group ministry leader. Sometimes bringing in someone outside the group provides the remedy that was elusive up to that point.

Whatever method or approach you use to deal with difficulties, be sure to involve the members of your group. Group problems must be owned by every member and dealt with by all. Remember this, lack of *clarity* and lack of *charity* do the most to hinder the success of a small group.

TIPS

Here is a list of tips for dealing with group difficulties or conflict:

1. Attempt to define and describe the conflict in cooperative terms (as a common problem).

2. Try to deal with issues rather than personalities.
3. Deal with one issue at a time.
4. Attempt to persuade one another rather than using threats, intimidation, and power plays.
5. Focus on issues while they are small rather than permitting them to grow over time and become large ones.
6. Opt for full disclosure of all facts rather than allowing "hidden agendas" (leftover feelings or old arguments not settled) to function.
7. Encourage the validation of the other parties' interests or concerns (feelings are valid no matter what the facts are).
8. Emphasize what you still hold in common.
9. Attempt to portray a trusting and friendly attitude.
10. Opt for a "win-win" feeling (i.e., there is a piece of the pie for each one) rather than a "win-lose" feeling.
11. Attempt to generate as many new ideas and as much new information as possible in order to broaden the perspective of all persons involved.
12. Involve all principal parties in the conflict at a common meeting.
13. Clarify whether you are dealing with one conflict or multiple conflicts.[1]

In the *Small Group Leaders' Handbook,* Steve Barker presents a shorter but very helpful list:

1. Set a time for conflict (take time to deal with it, don't hide from conflict).
2. There should be no winner and no loser.
3. Every member, within the limits of time, should participate in some way.
4. Be critical of ideas and not people.
5. Members who disagree must achieve an understanding of both points of view.
6. Emotions are to be answered by emotions (how you feel about the situation).
7. Power should be balanced (everyone should have equal rights).[2]

PROBLEM PEOPLE

Earlier we discussed five typical problem areas and mentioned that most were actually people problems. One of these people problems is especially important to deal with, namely people's expectations for the group and the associated behavior. Meet some folks I have run into and you're likely to encounter, if you haven't done so already.

Social Sidney—Life of the party, that's Sid. He wants to "lighten up" the sessions and have some fun. Sid views the group as an opportunity to be with people, a context to meet his need for social involvement— even though he may not consciously recognize the fact. Sid merely puts up with the actual group meetings . . . any excuse to be with people he likes and needs.

Academic Ann—Ann is an intellectual giant who takes great pleasure in "digging" into Scripture. Her expectations for the small group are not met unless Bible study is the exclusive group activity. Every word in the Biblical passage must be carefully analyzed . . . in the original language. Interpreting the passage is her goal, its application and other members of the group are of little interest.

Listener Larry—Not much of a talker, Larry just wants to listen to what the others have to say. Mentally, he is actively involved. And on the rare occasion when he does speak, his comments usually are thoughtful and well-stated. Larry wants other group members to accept his quiet participation and leave him alone. He is always the first to leave at the end of the meeting.

Holy Harry—Harry is so heavenly minded his fellow group members question his earthly value. He's quick with spiritual clichés, fast to spout biblical platitudes. Harry has no personal problems or struggles. His holier-than-thou attitude turns off other group members. Harry's desire is for the group to focus on the heavenly and set aside the earthly.

Application Alice—"How does that apply to me?" is Alice's constant question. Too much time spent on interpreting and understanding the passage doesn't please her. During Bible studies she wants to quickly "experience the text" and draw out the application. For Alice, however, actually putting the application into *practice* isn't a big concern.

Philosopher Phil—Theology and philosophy are Phil's passions.

He wants the group to focus on "heavy" issues. A good group, according to him, is one that revolves around the leader lecturing on the intricacies of the topic or biblical passage. Group discussion is okay—if kept to a minimum—but he prefers debating philosophical issues with the leader.

Counselor Carol—Carol sees the group sessions through the eyes of a counselor. She "psychologizes" every topic, every discussion. Group members are treated like clients who are in desperate need of her counsel.

Counselee Clara—Clara is Carol's counterpart. She wants the group to serve as a therapy session. She desperately yearns for the group to study biblical passages that may give her a solution to one of her many problems.

Preacher Patrick—Every group session is Patrick's pulpit. He eagerly anticipates each meeting. Long hours are spent preparing. While not the official group leader, he dominates the discussion and, in effect, takes over. Patrick is well-meaning, but gets on the other members' nerves. His desire to strongly admonish group members stems from the fact that he was saved out of a tempestuous background, and now he wants to shield his friends from the agony he experienced.

Forced Frank—Frank doesn't have any expectations because he doesn't even want to be there. The truth be known, he attends only because he's feels forced to—by a demanding spouse, a craving to be accepted, some sort of ulterior motive, or another person or situation. There in body but not in mind or soul, Frank just wants to be left alone.

The characters introduced here are extreme cases. Their expectations are legitimate, but taken to eccentric ends. Most likely you don't have anyone in your group who precisely embodies one of these extremes, or let's hope not.

MANAGING EXPECTATIONS

Different expectations and perspectives can cause friction among the members of your group. It is important for you as a group leader to know about and be prepared to deal with these various expectations—to assure that all of the members benefit, including yourself.

Here are five methods to ward off potential problems by managing divergent expectations.

First, talk about your expectations. As in a strong marriage, group members need open communication. At one of the first sessions of your group you'd be wise to spend time talking about what each member expects from the experience. This is important because different expectations represent different needs. Not all needs can or should be met in one group. Help members evaluate their expectations in light of the purposes for which you are meeting.

Second, assist group members to formulate new, appropriate expectations. It is vital from the very beginning to clearly state the intended purposes for the group. This permits members to weigh their own expectations and make adjustments as necessary. In some cases it means helping group members to adopt new expectations.

The third method you can use to ward off potential problems is to periodically "test the water." Expectations change. This is true for each member and for the group as a whole. At regular intervals—maybe every two months—evaluate the group atmosphere to learn if expectations in the area of format, process, topic, and so on, have changed or been altered. If most of the members express new expectations, it may be appropriate to add, replace, or modify intended purposes for the group.

Fourth, speak in private with individual group members. Frequently, group discussions on the topic of expectations and behavior won't produce satisfactory self-analysis. Some of us just aren't capable of evaluating our own motivations. As a result, you'll occasionally have a participant who continues to display unsuitable attitudes, actions, and participation. I have found it worthwhile to go to that person, in private, and talk it through. Typically the person is unaware of his or her behavior and is quick to make the appropriate corrections.

An occasional member will have and continue to push expectations that are outside the bounds of your group. As a last resort, after all other avenues have been exhausted—for the benefit of all concerned—you may have to ask an uncooperative member to withdraw from the group. If it is necessary to do this, please deal with the person privately.

ARE YOU READY?

I've thrown a lot of advice at you. Are you ready to deal with group problems? Let's see. Carefully read each of the following situations. Determine what you think the problem is and how you would handle it. Since these are contrived examples (based on my experience), there are no absolute right answers. However, to help you evaluate your responses, suggested answers are on pages 112-114.

Problem Situations

1. During a lively group discussion you notice that the members are beginning to drift away from the topic of focus.
2. One group member has a tendency to speak for the whole group, saying things like, "We all know that . . ." or "Nobody believes that. . . ."
3. A question is asked by a group member, but the group moves on without giving consideration to the question.
4. The group consists of twelve members, yet only four people take an active part in the discussions.
5. A group member verbally attacks a suggestion given by another member.
6. Two group members become engaged in a heated argument.
7. A certain group member is prone to answer all questions and give comments on all issues.
8. Two close friends always sit together and have numerous side discussions.
9. One group member (the life of the party) is able to find humor in any situation and loudly shares it with everyone.
10. It has been three meetings since a normally active group member has been in attendance.
11. The group members cannot agree on the details of a proposed outing.
12. Regardless of the topic, this group member is able to turn the discussion to his pet interest, his problems.
13. The group is angry with a member who is constantly negative in her comments and assessment of people's attitudes and contributions.

Potential Responses

As you have already noticed, the situations lack certain background and descriptive information that would be very helpful in determining your actual responses if the cases were real. Nevertheless, here are generic answers, giving a definition of the problem and *possible* solutions. Do you agree?

These sample responses are based on two assumptions: (1) a group covenant exists (see pages 46-48), and (2) the suggested interventions are the joint responsibilities of both the leader and the members.

Problem 1: Losing focus, drifting discussion
Politely intervene and point out the drifting tendency. Call the group back to the topic. Determine if the group wishes to change directions and pursue the new topic and/or schedule it for a future meeting.

Problem 2: Personal opinions projected as group opinions
Often a friendly reminder to speak only for oneself is sufficient.

Problem 3: Failure to recognize a member's contribution
Call the group back to the unresolved question. Seek an answer or determine how and when an answer can be pursued (perhaps outside of the group). Affirm the questioner even though the question may not be appropriate.

Problem 4: Unbalanced participation patterns
Here are three of the many alternatives: Divide the group into smaller groups to discuss the issue, and then have each subgroup report to the whole group. Conclude your question to the group by saying, "Let's hear from someone who hasn't commented yet." It is often recommended to ask the silent members direct questions. I would avoid asking such questions until the group is well-established and a high comfort level exists.

Problem 5: Hostility toward a person's idea
Interrupt tactfully. Affirm the right to disagree. Remind both individuals of the participation standards outlined in the group's covenant. Suggest whatever restitution is necessary to calm feelings.

Problem 6: Violent disagreement turns into a combative situation
Shoot them both . . . just kidding. Intervene, follow the four-step strategy for problem solving. Remind the group of your participation covenant. If necessary, deal with the situation at another time outside of the group meeting.

Problem 7: Member dominates group discussions
Talk with the person in private. Ask for his assistance in allowing others to participate. In extreme cases, while affirming the value of his participation, ask the person to consciously limit his verbal responses.

Problem 8: Members' lack of group etiquette
Redirect the two members' attention to the group activity. Ask them to share their insight with the whole group. Set up physical conditions that prevent them from sitting together. Break into subgroups to separate them. Talk with each of them outside of the group meetings, if the behavior persists.

Problem 9: Inappropriate timing and use of humor
Talk with the person in private. He may not realize the problem he's creating. You'll probably need to have more than one private discussion.

Problem 10: Poor attendance
Contact the person on the telephone. Determine the cause for being absent. If the reason is legitimate, express concern, ask if assistance is needed, and state your anticipation of the person's return. If the reason is questionable, remind the member of the group covenant, express a desire for active participation, and highlight the person's importance to the group.

Problem 11: Disagreement over activity
Look for a compromise solution. Compromise is legitimate when issues of choice are at stake, but not in matters of doctrine. If a compromise cannot be reached, postpone the decision and look for other alternatives.

Problem 12: Inappropriate expectations
Talk with the person outside of the group. Explore the possibility of securing professional counseling. Encourage the other group members to support this member outside the group meetings.

Problem 13: Conflict over personal behavior
Have the group gently confront the person with her behavior. Care must be exercised to avoid the appearance of attacking the member. Review the applicable items within the group covenant. Some type of interaction with the person outside the group meetings is likely.

CONSTRUCTIVE CONFLICT

Let me briefly mention the constructive use of conflict: staged conflict used to stimulate discussion and cause group members to think and act. The group that sails along with its members always giving the "right" answers may be the group that isn't thinking.

At times it is profitable to discuss controversial issues in order to create a controlled conflict. Very worthwhile exchanges can take place after an issue or question introduces tension and disagreement. When this happens, you can point the members to the Word of God as the final authority, instead of tradition or merely logical reasoning.

Controlled conflict is best introduced by using confrontation questions. Here are some examples.

Questions that require a decision—Which is better, to do what is right when you don't feel like it, or wait to act until you have the right motive, feeling, or desire?

Questions that imply something that is not true—Why might we say that Muhammad was the greatest man who ever lived?

Controversial questions—Why does God allow suffering? Is there a biblical basis for ordaining women? Should Christians join the military forces?

When introducing conflict, stay in control. It is easy to let things get out of hand. The aim should be to move the discussion to an examination of God's Word. Sometimes it's important for the group to realize that God's Word doesn't give a specific answer but allows room for different opinions.

Of course, you must be cautious when using confrontation

questions. Animosity, division, and strife can result if you're not careful. Wait to use constructive conflict until the group is well-established and the members have developed strong relationships. Then, acknowledging the controversy in the topic is an important initial step. When wrapping up the discussion, make sure the biblical solutions or principles are emphasized.[3]

NOTES:

1. Based on Nathan Turner, *Effective Leadership in Small Groups* (Judson Press, 1977).
2. Adapted from Steve Barker, *Small Group Leaders' Handbook* (InterVarsity Press, 1982).
3. Portions of this section were adapted from *How to Lead Small Group Bible Studies* (Colorado Springs, Colo.: NavPress, 1982), pages 43-45.

CHAPTER SEVEN

Evaluating
Your Group

E valuation is an everyday occurrence. You and I are constantly evaluating the people, products, events, and organizations we encounter. We go about this process consciously and
unconsciously. Our judgments range from instantaneous emotional
reactions to careful reflections. Most frequently our evaluations are
random or *informal* in nature. They are quickly exercised and just as
quickly lost.

This type of informal evaluation is also a fact of life within our
small groups. Informal evaluations happen because groups are made
up of individual people, and people naturally pass judgment on their
surroundings. As group members, we are constantly "checking out"
each other and the group's processes and activities. Some good things
can come from these informal assessments, but typically the potential
benefits aren't captured and used.

Consequently, the judgments made in informal evaluations
within groups aren't sufficient for making necessary decisions and
changes. For evaluation to have its greatest benefit it must be carefully
thought out and implemented. We need a formal systematic procedure.
I use the word *formal* here to denote organization and purposefulness,
not rigidity or ritualism.

This chapter is designed to briefly guide you through the rationale and steps for conducting a formal evaluation of your group.
Quality small groups, in my opinion, will not happen without formal
evaluation.

WHAT IS EVALUATION?

Evaluation is one of those words that seems to have a different shade of meaning for every person. How would you define it? You aren't alone if you struggle in coming up with a clear definition. Even the experts aren't able to agree.

For our purposes, evaluation is *the systematic process of obtaining information and using it to form judgments, which in turn are used in decision making.*

To illustrate, you make an evaluation before you decide to cancel or alter a group activity, or when you assess the level of relationships that exist among the members. You participate in the evaluation process when you pick the best day and time to meet, or when you select a Bible study workbook to use. All these examples encompass obtaining information, forming judgments, and making decisions.

Information: essential ingredient—Information is the necessary component in making judgments. It may come in many ways and have many forms. It is the raw material on which evaluations are based. Timely, accurate information undergirds judgments that lead to logical decisions.

For example, this is the typical type of information you may need in making judgments and, finally, decisions:

♦ Four group members dropped out of the group after three months, but continue to attend other church activities.
♦ More than half of the group members have expressed their dissatisfaction with the group's unchanging format.
♦ Now that the group has ended, members still want to spend time together and assist each other.

Judgment: initial determination—With accurate and timely information in hand, you think about what it means and form a judgment. Judgments are opinions or informed estimates based on the available facts. They are initial determinations (preliminary decisions) upon which final decisions are based. Specifically, judgments are estimates of the present situation or predictions of future performance. More than one judgment is possible given the specific information. Here are possible judgments based on the previous examples of information:

> ♦ Four members have withdrawn from the group without stating their reasons for doing so. I have waited too long to find out why.
> ♦ Boredom is setting in. The group members dislike doing the same thing at every meeting.
> ♦ Our group was successful in facilitating strong, helping relationships.

Decisions: final outcome—Decision making is the concluding step in formal evaluation. In effect, decisions are rulings or the *actions* to be taken based on the related judgment. A judgment may lead to one or more decisions. You want to make rational, reasonable choices based on the judgment you've made, which are the logical products of reliable information. Staying on track with the prior examples, here are some possible decisions:

> ♦ I must contact the former members and determine why they chose to withdraw from the group.
> ♦ A format change is needed—explore alternatives at our next meeting.
> ♦ The group was successful. We should expand the number of groups offered.

Information, judgments, and decisions are the essence of formal evaluation. But they alone aren't what make evaluations successful. All the correct theory and technique, while important, isn't going to amount to much if you don't have a servant's heart. As the leader, your attitude is the most important ingredient when evaluating small groups.

WHY EVALUATION?

The answer to the question "Why do evaluations?" is obvious to some and puzzling to others. Can you think of reasons why the evaluation process should be implemented in your group? Here are my ideas.

We have a biblical mandate. The most compelling reason I can offer as a rationale for doing evaluation is found in the Bible. Now, evaluating your group isn't expressly commanded. However, the idea or principle of evaluation is clearly taught in Scripture. Words such as *judge, test,* and *examine* are used to convey the idea.

- ◆ A plea for God's evaluation (Psalm 26:2).
- ◆ One day we will experience God's ultimate evaluation (Psalm 96:13).
- ◆ We should avoid evaluating a weaker brother's opinions (Romans 14:1).
- ◆ We are to engage in self-evaluation (2 Corinthians 13:5).
- ◆ We are to evaluate our own work (Galatians 6:4).
- ◆ God evaluates our hearts (1 Thessalonians 2:4).
- ◆ We are to evaluate all things (1 Thessalonians 5:21).
- ◆ The Bible evaluates our thoughts and intentions (Hebrews 4:12).
- ◆ Teachers will receive a stricter evaluation (James 3:1).

But wait a minute! What about Luke 6:37, "Do not judge, and you will not be judged. Do not condemn, and you will not be condemned. Forgive, and you will be forgiven." Is this verse telling us *not* to evaluate? A casual glance might lead us to think so. However, this isn't the meaning of the verse. Looking at the context, we learn that the issue in question was an attitude of seeking to condemn or find fault. Love and correct knowledge were totally lacking. In Luke 6:37, Jesus is forbidding self-righteous, self-appointed judgment of others in place of God's evaluation. This verse pictures evaluation at its worst. It is the opposite of our current discussion.

Evaluation promotes quality. Quality, effective small groups don't just happen. Evaluation is a tool to assist you in meeting your goals and instigating change when it is needed. Too often we merely assume all is going well or that we are doing the best job possible. Honest evaluation helps us to check out these assumptions and, if we find them in error, alerts us to the necessary changes needed.

Evaluation builds in accountability. We all need to be held accountable for the responsibilities and tasks we undertake. Even if you're only answerable to yourself, evaluation provides a means to assess your progress. Remember, our ultimate accountability is to God. Everything we do must be done well. We serve the King!

Evaluation provides the basis for making responsible decisions. From a pragmatic perspective, this idea is an important justification undergirding evaluation. Flimsy information and snap judgments produce poor decisions. On the other hand, decisions based on the results of a formal evaluation—rather than hearsay or personal bias—provide the sound basis for choosing between alternatives. Furthermore, when asked to explain your decisions, you'll have logical reasons to offer.

WHY NOT EVALUATION?

Not everyone is keen on evaluation. There is a strong possibility that someone within your group, or a church leader outside your small group, will object to your evaluation efforts. To prepare you for potential dissent, let me share five common reasons why people are apprehensive about or discount the need for evaluation in small group ministries.

They fear negative results. From their perspective, evaluation is designed to find fault and place blame. They think the goal is to discover and criticize those things they are doing wrong.

They think evaluation is a waste of time. Since everything is moving along so great, why go to all the time and bother? They feel that evaluation is not needed. The time spent evaluating is better utilized doing something more productive.

They believe you can't evaluate spiritual matters. Many see evaluation as a worldly concept. As such, they argue that it is foreign to biblical ideals and Christian activities.

They have anxiety over the process. They commonly say, "I can't do it, I don't know how. Where do I start? What if I make a mistake?"

They feel political pressure. Unfortunately, politics exists even in the church. Your evaluation may not serve the purposes of some person or group. Pressure is exerted, and you're given some excuse why an evaluation should not be conducted.

To be successful in evaluating your group, you need to help the members, and others, work through these and other fears they may have. Evaluation *can* help us to have better groups. But don't assume that everyone is ready and eager to evaluate. Go slowly, address everyone's fears, help others to understand and catch the vision for formal evaluation.

WHEN DO YOU EVALUATE?

Planning for evaluation should begin as early as possible, perhaps even before the group's first meeting. Having a well-thought-out plan greatly assists the implementation of your evaluation. But when do you put the actual plan into action?

Formal evaluation can be implemented at two different times or levels: (1) during the life of the group and (2) as a final activity as the group is drawing to a close. These two stages of formal evaluation are referred to as *formative* and *summative* evaluation.

Formative Evaluation

Formative evaluation refers to making decisions about small group relationships, processes, and activities while they are still capable of being modified. The formative evaluator gathers information and judges the merits of various aspects of the group in order to make improvements. Examples of still pliable group characteristics that a formative evaluation might bring to the surface include (1) administrative details, such as day, time, place, and meeting format, or (2) the relationships that are being nurtured in the group. Your intention is to assess such items in order to determine how your group can improve during its remaining weeks or months.

Therefore, the heart of a formative evaluation strategy is to gather reliable information regarding the effectiveness of various aspects of the group's life and activities while it is still functioning. This information provides the basis for making judgments and decisions about facets of the group that should continue and/or those aspects of the group that need adjustment or, if necessary, cancellation.

There is no set time to conduct a formative evaluation. But like most things, it is possible to overevaluate or underevaluate. Overevaluation usually isn't a problem, however. It is wise to set aside a specific amount of time to evaluate during several meetings throughout the life of the group.

Summative Evaluation

Summative evaluation refers to making decisions about the relationships, processes, and activities that took place in a group that is about to end or has ended. In conducting a summative evaluation you gather information and make judgments about the overall merits of the small group. This leads to decisions regarding the results, benefits, and needed improvements in future groups, or ultimately, whether or not to abandon small groups altogether. Whereas a formative evaluation is intended to inform the leader and the group members, a summative evaluation is most often geared toward the types of information helpful to the group's church or organizational sponsor.

The summative evaluator would, for instance, gather evidence in order to help management decide whether or not a specific group, once completed, has accomplished its intended purpose. The information might also help the leadership decide whether or not to continue funding and offering a small groups' program. A summative evaluation's bottom line is to help leaders decide if the program contributed to the organization's objectives.

The Evaluator's Role

In considering the distinction between these two evaluation emphases, it should be apparent that formative evaluation is far more partisan to the group. Your efforts should be aimed at doing everything in your power to help your group succeed. You aren't a distant, aloof judge. You are a member of the group, trying to make it a profitable experience for everyone. In contrast, when doing summative evaluation you should try not to have an overly partisan mindset, avoid the tendency to be influenced by the desire to make the group and yourself, as the leader of the group, look good. With a bit of valid trepidation, summative evaluation should be equated with the final judgment of your group.

It is possible, when performing either type of evaluation, for individuals other than the leader to conduct the process. There are advantages to having *external* versus *internal* evaluators in some situations. In general, external evaluators are more neutral, less influenced by personal associations with the group and its members, and as a result are more objective in their judgment. On the other hand, external evaluators frequently don't have a good perspective on the relationships that exist in the group, the group's developmental history, or knowledge of improvements the group has experienced over the course of its life. Consequently, I've found that external evaluators work best in summative contexts, while internal evaluators are superior for conducting formative evaluations. However, in many cases you or another member of your group are able to serve in both roles.

One real issue in both formative and summative evaluation is intimately associated with your church's organizational structure. That is, how much authority (the right to make decisions) do you really have? In your role as evaluator you must determine what decision-making structures—lines of accountability—exist within your church and must be observed. You may be allowed to make certain adjustments within your own group, but have little or no say in the overall groups' ministry, if one exists. In other situations, you may have complete freedom in your group and in sharing your ideas about the overall organization of the groups' ministry.

The best time to conduct a summative evaluation is during the last two or three group meetings, just before the group ends. Make it a positive experience, helping the group conclude on a positive note.

WHO OR WHAT DO YOU EVALUATE?

At least four areas, perhaps more, can become the focus of your evaluation. Two of these areas are straight forward and routine. The other two are a bit more touchy to deal with. Let's consider the more easily assessed aspects of your group first.

Details—Here the evaluation focuses on the suitability of the day, time, and place the group meets. Using a formative evaluation, you seek to make decisions on whether or not adjustments in these details are needed.

Often the details aren't flexible. The group was established around certain specifics. The members elected to be part of the group because they could fit the details of the meetings into their schedules. This suggests that in some cases a formative evaluation isn't necessary. Changing the details isn't an option. In situations like this, valuable feedback comes from your summative evaluation. Should the same details be used again, or what changes are needed the next time?

Format—Two sub-elements need to be addressed when making decisions about your group's format: (1) how the allotted amount of time is divided and (2) the specific activities within the time structure. The structuring of your time is an important stewardship. You want to know if the way you divide your time is effective. Is more time needed for some activities and/or less for others? Then within the divisions, the examination of the specific activities is next. Is the Bible study, discussion, prayer, task, process, and so on, satisfactory? What is working and can continue with no changes? What isn't working and needs changes or minor alterations to enhance the well-being of the group?

The next two important dimensions of your group should be included in your evaluation. To leave them out would seriously limit the evaluation's quality. They are people considerations. As such, they are more susceptible to producing misunderstandings and hurt feelings. Before you discount this, you need to know that the final item deals with you, the leader of the group.

Relationships—Interpersonal relationships are important to the success of every group, regardless of its purpose or type. How people treat one another, communicate, express care for one another, share personal issues, and so on, must be judged. Your examination of these aspects is a vital factor in the evaluation process.

While evaluating relationships within all groups is important, within process-oriented groups it is the major concern. Relationships are the reason why this type of group exists. Your evaluation efforts, therefore, must begin with a well-organized formative evaluation. You cannot wait for the summative evaluation.

Leadership—Perhaps no single element has greater influence on the success of the group than does leadership. You as the leader set the tone, model the process, suggest the alternatives, guide the decision-making process, motivate the members, arrange the details, and so on. All these aspects or group tasks should be evaluated using both formative and summative strategies.

Before you faint at the idea of being evaluated, remember that you aren't the only focus in a leadership evaluation. In chapter 2, I suggested that a group should seek to achieve shared leadership. Not that the designated leader is no longer necessary, but that healthy groups become responsible for their own self-leadership. Consequently, any evaluation of leadership that neglects to examine shared leadership is shortsighted and incomplete.

HOW DO YOU EVALUATE?

Talking about evaluation is a lot easier than doing it. Therefore, if you are to go beyond words and become a successful evaluator, you need tools. Your first and most important tool is a model to escort you through the evaluation process. A model is simply an idealized plan of action. It provides a carefully thought out set of procedures to guide your efforts.

Many times, however, every step in the model need not be carried out to its fullest detail. Individual situations require different approaches. So, it may be preferable to omit certain steps or complete others out of sequence. A model is merely a guide, not a set of rigid requirements.

Whether you're conducting a formative evaluation or wrapping up your group with a summative evaluation, you'll go through three basic phases:

The Planning Phase: Preparing to Evaluate
The Process Phase: Acquiring the Needed Information
The Product Phase: Making and Communicating
      Judgments and Decisions

I've already alluded to most of the activities included in the three phases. But to solidify your understanding, it's helpful to examine each phase, taking it apart and putting it back together again. Each phase can be divided into a number of steps. When the phases and steps are combined, you have a useful evaluation model.

Although more than one model exists, I'm partial to my adaptation of a model developed by Terry D. TenBrink in *Evaluation: A Practical Guide for Teachers.* I've used this ten-step model many times. It works! Here's my adapted model.

THE PLANNING PHASE: PREPARING TO EVALUATE

The planning phase consists of the first five steps in the following ten-step model. They organize your evaluation and precede the actual gathering of information. The purpose of this phase is to determine what you want to do and how you plan to do it.

Step One: State the Decisions or Questions You Want to Make.

The importance of this first step cannot be over stressed. Unless you clearly specify the decisions you want or need to make, proceeding is very difficult, if not impossible. The information to be gathered and the subsequent judgments to be made are very much dependent on what decisions you are facing. In effect, you are working backward. By first identifying the nature of the decision(s)—without making the actual decision—you set up a framework that dictates the information needed and the type of judgments necessary.

At the beginning of this chapter, we learned that decisions are rulings or the actions to be taken based on the related judgments. The goal is to make rational, reasonable choices from among clearly identified choices.

By now you should be asking yourself, "How is this done?" Step one is most easily accomplished by formulating questions. Questions set up the kinds of decisions that are pursued in the evaluation. Questions reflect the areas in which decisions are needed. For example:

- ◆ Was the starting time for the group okay?
- ◆ Did the members enjoy being a group?
- ◆ How does each member feel about his or her participation in the group?
- ◆ What can I do to improve as a discussion leader?

The questions may come from different sources. You can identify questions based on the four potential areas of group evaluation discussed earlier. The questions may come from a set of ideal criteria or standards you previously identified when you planned your group, you may want to ask your group members for suggestions, or the questions may come from your own experience. No one source is best.

The questions may be very specific or more general in nature. If you want a detailed evaluation, you'll identify very detailed questions. A more general or casual evaluation is a product of general, less specific questions. These questions can often be answered simply yes or no. The first two question examples suggest a more casual approach. The second two would lend themselves to being part of a detailed assessment.

Step Two: Describe the Needed Information.
You already know that information is the substance from which judgments and decisions are made. But what is information itself? The answer may seem obvious. Information is the acquired data or facts that supply answers to your questions. Every question states, or at least implies, the kind of information it would take to answer it.

Step two is so apparent it's easily overlooked. Nevertheless, it is wise to jot down the specific information you need. Four guidelines can provide a path for you to identify this information.

First, the information must be *first-hand.* Information gathered directly from the source is preferred. Second-hand information, what you are told about how someone else feels, flirts with misunderstanding or just plain error. Yet, at times you may have to use second-hand information. If this is the case, my advice is to always avoid third- or fourth-hand information.

Second, the data and facts must be *current.* Making judgments and decisions on information that was true six months ago is risky, it may not still be current. Therefore, either check its present status or secure new information.

Third, the information must be *complete.* Securing all available data is a must. Many seemingly good decisions will later be found lacking if they have been based on incomplete information. Even just one or two absent pieces of data could change the outcome completely.

And fourth, it must be *accurate* information. The accuracy of your information is very important. Even if the data is current and complete, inaccuracy nullifies its usefulness. Precise, reliable information is the basis for quality decisions.

First-hand, current, complete, and accurate information is the goal. Without all four of these characteristics your information is ineffectual for decision making. Of course, useless information quickly derails your evaluation.

Based on the examples of questions previously given, this is the type of information that's likely needed for your evaluation.

Was the starting time for the group okay?—You could check attendance records (if they exist), ask personal statements of the members, and/or recall the number of times people arrived late. What additional information do you think would be of value?

Did the group enjoy being a group?—Start with the members' personal opinions. Secondary evidence, such as casual comments you've heard expressed by the members or the number of times members sought to meet together outside of the regular group meetings, may also be helpful, if accurate.

How does each member feel about his or her participation in the group?—The necessary information is pretty straightforward. You'll need to get each member's feedback.

What can I do to improve as a discussion leader?—Here again, input from your group members is useful. However, you may also need to go to outside sources, such as books or magazine articles, to gather information on the characteristics of an effective discussion leader.

Step Three: Locate Any Information Available.
In some cases portions of the information you need may already exist. Your task becomes one of determining if such information in fact exists and whether or not it's something you'll need.

Examples of existing information that may be of help include attendance records, summaries of previous formative evaluations, the group's covenant, written statements of the group's goals, or group guidelines provided by your church.

Existing information is more frequently used in evaluations of an entire small groups' ministry, rather than in the evaluation of an individual group. However, this doesn't mean that such information cannot be made useful to you. At this point, our model calls for you to make that determination.

Returning to the four questions we are using to illustrate this discussion—questions that primarily focus on the evaluation of one group—I'd suggest that existing information probably isn't a major factor. Why? Because most individual groups don't keep records, unless required to do so as part of participating in a larger groups' ministry within their church.

**Step Four: Determine How, Where, and When
to Obtain Needed Information.**

In most cases the primary and best source of evaluation information
is the group members. Go ahead, ask them! But first determine how,
where, and when. There are no simple, required answers here. So,
let's look at the possible options you have to choose from.

How?—The first thing to nail down is how you will go about
getting the information you've identified as necessary. The two most
common methods of collecting evaluative information within groups
are *observation* and *inquiry*.

Inquiry means you ask. By asking, you can get a great deal of
first-hand information. When you want to know what a person or
group is thinking, ask. Realize, however, that information gained
in this manner is highly subjective and open to distortion. Most
people—including you and me—want to look good in the eyes of
others. People often tend to answer questions in a manner that meets
this need. Or, they give an answer that isn't necessarily a personal
opinion, but it is what they think you want. As time passes and
the group relationships become more secure, the amount of such
distortion declines. You might want to consider, if time and other
resources permit, supplementing inquiry information with careful,
systematic observation.

Observation is the process of looking and listening. You carefully and systematically observe to collect information and/or confirm
information already in hand. Observe behaviors or skills such as
listening, carrying out instructions, responding to needs, genuine-
ness of a comment, receptivity to a divergent opinion, and so on.
These behaviors cannot be assessed adequately with pencil and paper
questionnaires or rating forms, but they can be measured quite well
through skillful observation.

Once you determine the general information-gathering method
you want to use, then you need to decide exactly how you will
proceed. Would a questionnaire work? How about a rating scale?
Is conducting an interview with a checklist the best strategy?

The interview and questionnaire are the two most useful tools
for gathering information through inquiry.

Interviews—The evaluator verbally asks a series of questions
and records the answers. This provides valuable first-hand infor-

mation about opinions, interests, reactions, attitudes, behavior, and self-perceptions. Interviews are possible with individual members and/or groups. The results rest on the skills of the interviewer. A major disadvantage is that information gathered in this fashion is open to the interviewer's interpretative error.

A slight variation of the interview is the group discussion. The major distinction between this and a straight interview is the level of formality used to conduct the process. Discussions are usually more casual and less structured than interviews.

Written responses—A written response is used to get feedback directly from the group members in written form. A questionnaire of some kind is used most routinely. However, evaluation forms that include statements to be ranked, items to be checked, or sentences to be completed are among the other possibilities. Written response strategies are well-suited to obtaining personal facts and information about attitudes, opinions, and some self-reported behaviors. Potential disadvantages include the fact that people often don't tell the truth, leave incomplete answers, and the real problem, poorly designed questionnaires.

If you wish to gather your evaluative information through observation, here are some options:

Anecdotal records—These are factual, written descriptions of observations. This is time consuming and depends on the observer's observation skills.

Checklists—A list of specific items is used, marking them off as they are observed, and/or tallying the frequency of their occurrence.

Rating scales—Make a set of characteristics or statements to serve as criteria for judgment. The observer uses the scale to indicate the degree of acceptable or unacceptable characteristics observed. For example, suppose you are observing verbal patterns using a scale of one to five, with one denoting unacceptable behavior and five, highly desirable behavior. If a group member lashes out at another member, you would record a one or a two, depending on the severity of the incident.

Rankings—A fairly crude observation tool, rankings ask the observer to rank various aspects of the group from members to activities, and so on, according to some standard that often is vague. Because ranking is inaccurate, it is best used only in situations where accurate information is not an important issue and rough estimates are sufficient.

Most of the techniques used in observation can also be used as inquiry methods. The difference is how the methods are administered. In observation the evaluator records the information, and those being evaluated may or may not know about the process. (Knowing they are being observed may cause problems. They could behave in ways unrepresentative of their normal behavior. But if they find out later they were evaluated without their knowledge you may have even greater problems.) In inquiry the group members almost always know that an evaluation is being conducted and record the information for themselves (except in an interview).

WHERE and WHEN?—In the vast majority of cases, it is best to collect the needed information during one of your regular group meetings. Information required for formative evaluations can be sought several times throughout the year. An entire group session isn't needed, but allow adequate time. In doing so you communicate the importance of evaluation.

Use one or two meetings toward the final weeks of your group to obtain summative evaluation information. Here again, the whole session is not needed, unless you choose to use a discussion-interview format.

Some group leaders prefer not to use part of their group's meeting time to secure the needed information. They ask the members to fill out the evaluation questionnaire at home and bring it to the next meeting. This alternative hasn't worked well for me. Too often some people forget to complete the form, lose it, or neglect to bring it back. Maybe your results would be better than mine.

The timing of the information gathering is very important. Schedule dates and times that do not cause conflict or hardship on the group as a whole or its individual members. For example, it may not be a good idea to pass out an unannounced, lengthy questionnaire at a group meeting when the members have planned to spend the entire time in prayer. Simply put, no surprises!

Finally, pay attention to the details of data gathering. If you are seeking a written response, be sure to have extra pencils on hand, something for the members to write on, and obviously, enough copies of the evaluation form.

Step Five: Develop Your Information Gathering Tool.
Step five involves translating your decision on how to gather the information you need into an actual data-gathering tool. Don't let the word *tool* throw you. It is typically used to describe questionnaires, rating sheets, feedback forms, and so on.

A well-designed tool is essential to obtaining needed information. Realistically, the topic of making evaluation tools is too large to tackle within the confines of this book and isn't necessary. Let me suggest a few things to help you succeed in developing an adequate evaluation questionnaire.

Decide on a response strategy—Decide what response strategy is best suited for getting the type of information you need. For example, if you use a questionnaire, are you going to use open-ended questions (blank space to write an answer) or structured choice questions (select a provided answer)?

Write carefully—Take care in writing your questions or response items. An effective tool is made up of good items. Formulating this is not as easy as you may think. Writing questionnaires or evaluation forms takes knowledge, skill, and practice. Judge what you write for clarity and conciseness. One trick is to ask yourself, "How can a person misread or misanswer this item?"

Write out instructions—Written instructions tell the group members what they are being asked to do. Your goal is clear, specific, and understandable instructions. A good way to check these qualities is to have someone read the instructions and then verbally tell you what he thinks is supposed to be done. The person's response quickly tells you if your instructions work.

Quality appearance—Use care and quality in reproducing and assembling your tool. Many times the paper color, spacing, print size, and length affect the results you'll get. The physical appearance of the form says a lot about how important evaluation is to you and the group.

A few comments on finding published evaluation forms. I know of no valid and reliable small group evaluation forms available for you to buy and use. But given the increasing interest in small groups, it is very likely some are on their way. If this happens, please use caution with such tools. Carefully determine if the content of the tool matches your situation. Most of these forms are generic; they are written with a middle of the road situation in mind. Ask yourself if the questions, response items, ratings, and so on, reflect your group. Final decisions based on any such tools should be held tentatively. Another option you may want to consider is rewriting the form in order to tailor it to your own needs.

THE PROCESS PHASE: ACQUIRING THE NEEDED INFORMATION

With your evaluation well-planned, now it's time to actually obtain, analyze, and record the information you desire. This is the action phase of the evaluation. It will run smoothly if you did your homework in the first phase.

Step Six: Obtain the Needed Information.

Put your plan into action. Make certain you are thoroughly familiar with the procedures you plan to use and have all the materials you need at hand.

It is smart to make certain the group members, your source of information, are prepared. Dropping a questionnaire on them unannounced, not informing them of what you intend to do with the information, or threatening them with negative aspects of evaluation are examples of poor implementation.

Stay realistic. Sometimes, even though you're well-prepared and do everything right (at least in your own eyes), the results turn out to be less than what you expect. Chalk it up to experience and give it another try, being careful to avoid repeating any mistakes a second time.

Step Seven: Record the Information.

Now that you have the information you need, what are you going to do with it? First, you need to be sure that the information is credible for making the upcoming judgments or decisions. Do you recall the guidelines for good data? You want information that is *first-hand, current, complete,* and *accurate.* If your data cannot pass these standards, go back and collect information that does.

Recording information is the process of arranging data in an organized, written, and usable format. You are writing your results.

Data from questionnaires and interviews needs tabulation. Records of your information may be in the form of words or numbers. If you're using a personal computer, create a data file. In addition, your written organization of the information produces a file record of your results.

The long and the short of it is that you must translate the raw data you received during the collection phase into information that can be used to make judgments and decisions. This needn't be an overly difficult task in most cases.

THE PRODUCT PHASE: MAKING AND COMMUNICATING JUDGMENTS AND DECISIONS

You've reached the final phase. Now come the formal judgments and decisions based on the information you've organized. Most likely, you've already formed preliminary judgments and considered possible decisions. Be careful! Don't fall into the trap of fixing the evaluation to confirm your previously held opinions and attitudes.

Evaluation demands well thought out, sound judgments and decisions. This last phase is extremely important! Go slow, do a good job, and weigh the alternatives carefully.

Step Eight: Make Judgments.

Remember that judgments are opinions or informed estimates based on available facts. They are initial determinations (preliminary decisions) upon which final decisions are based. Specifically, judgments are estimates of the present situation or predictions of future performance.

Suppose you are considering the decision reflected in the evaluative question, "Did the members enjoy being a group?" Based on the information you recorded in step seven, now you form judgments. Notice that I said *judgments*. Usually it takes more than one judgment before any given decision is made.

Let's assume the necessary information has been collected and recorded. You could possibly make the following judgments:

♦ On a scale from one to ten, with ten being the highest level of agreement, six was the average score for the second item on the evaluation questionnaire. This item asked for a response to the statement, "I liked memorizing two Bible verses each week" (information). A variation in opinion exists, not everyone liked the requirement (judgment).

◆ During a discussion that focused on evaluating the group, one member expressed tremendous frustration with how the group selected its format. No one else felt this was a problem (information). It is unlikely that this issue was a significant negative factor for a majority of the group members (judgment).

◆ On the evaluation questionnaire, eleven of twelve group members ranked "New Friendships" as number one from among ten options describing potential benefits of group membership (information). The primary benefit of being a group member is the opportunity to establish new friendships (judgment).

Step Nine: Make Decisions.

The ultimate reason for evaluation is to make informed decisions. We know that a decision is the ruling or action to be taken based on rational, reasonable choices. These choices, based on the judgments you've made, are the logical products of reliable information.

Every evaluation decision you make as a group leader should be carefully and systematically worked through. You will find that no matter how carefully you approach decision making, you cannot make good decisions if you are working with faulty judgments. Don't fail to ask yourself, "Are my judgments and the information they are based on as accurate as possible?" (Review step two.)

If your answer is no, go back and obtain new information and reform your judgments. An alternate to this is to go ahead and make the decision, but be ready to alter it if the judgments prove to be less accurate than you first thought. There is nothing wrong with reversing an unsound decision. Doing so is a mark of integrity.

A systematic sub-model for making decisions is helpful. Here is a simple four-part decision-making process.

Review your decision objectives—If you're not certain of what you want your decision to accomplish, you'll likely fluctuate among many possible choices. You won't have a basis for selection. Review the decisions or questions you stipulated in step one of the evaluation model. By now—at the end of the process—you can fully appreciate why that first step was so important.

Identify possible decision alternatives—For every judgment a number of potential decisions exist. These alternatives are sometimes straightforward and easy to identify. At other times, they require careful research and/or talking with a number of people. Identifying every logical alternative is the ideal. However, don't overdo it. Concentrate on those choices that are realistic in your situation. (Review step eight.)

Weigh the consequences—This third stage goes hand in hand with previous stages. Each alternative identified has its own consequences. At this point, it is important to consider these questions: Which alternative is most suited to your objectives? Which results are you able to manage? Are any of the consequences totally unacceptable? You need only consider those consequences that are real possibilities.

Choose the best alternative—This is where everything is brought together. Now you (and/or the group) must decide on the most suitable course of action from among the alternatives. You recognize the probable outcomes and potential consequences. As in every major decision, you spend time in prayer asking for God's direction. A decision must be made . . . make it.

Please keep several things in mind as you make evaluative decisions. First, you may not have the freedom to make all the decisions. If your group is part of a larger groups' ministry, many decisions must be made by leaders overseeing the entire program. What may be good for your group, may not fit the overall goals and objectives of the larger program. Second, at times you may elect to make decisions that aren't warranted by the information, but you know it is the right thing to do. This situation may arise in cases where biblical standards are being questioned or principles of group dynamics are at stake.

And finally, your values play an important role in many decisions. Not your moral values necessarily, but your sense of priorities about what is most important, what must be done, and so on. Those things you value will get the most attention or consideration when you are choosing between alternatives. Therefore, it is important for you to be very alert to the values and opinions you hold and how they are reflected in your various decisions.

Step Ten: Communicate Decisions.
Who needs to know about your evaluation results? Normally, you'll need to communicate on several levels. Your group members no doubt want some immediate verbal feedback. A written record of the evaluation is also a smart idea. Are you required to submit a written report to someone outside of your group—a pastor or groups' ministry leader for example? Written or verbal reports should clearly identify the focus of the evaluation and why it was undertaken, your sources of information, the major decisions that were made (or need to be made by higher authorities), and the information and judgments behind the decisions.

A well-written evaluation document is worth the effort. It not only provides information for present actions, but it can also serve you in making future judgments and decisions. It can help you support your decisions to others. And certainly, a well-constructed report is one way to double check yourself, to make sure you've done a thorough job.

EVALUATION TIPS

Evaluation is both an art and a science. As a science it can be carefully studied, organized, examined, planned, defined, and refined. Yet, as an art a successful evaluation is also the result of a liberal amount of personal craftsmanship and finesse. With this in mind, here are a few tips I'd like to offer:

 ◆ Formal evaluation yields the best results when it is permeated with prayer and sensitivity to the Holy Spirit's direction.
 ◆ Formal evaluation is a process, not a single act. It involves a series of defined steps. Adequate time must be invested in conscientiously planning and conducting the process.
 ◆ Formal evaluation must involve the group members. Quality results are more likely if your fellow members have an active part in the evaluation process.
 ◆ Formal evaluation is a tool to help you, not a rope to bind you. Relax. Allow it to serve you and your group. The model you learned in this chapter may be applied with varying degrees of rigor.

♦ Formal evaluation is an idea that needs to be sold. Many people are afraid of evaluation because they see it as a fault-finding activity. How you go about presenting the idea is very important. Help your group members see it as an opportunity for further growth and development as individuals and as a group.

NOTE:
1. Ten-step model adapted from a model developed by Terry D. TenBrink, *Evaluation: A Practical Guide for Teachers* (Columbia, Mo.: The University of Missouri, 1974).

Epilogue

We've come to the end of our quick examination of your role as a small group leader. I trust it was a profitable journey. Thank you for allowing me the opportunity to share my opinions and experience with you.

To sum up, I'd like to share one final list of suggestions:

- Cling to the power of the Holy Spirit.
- Be patient with yourself, the members of your group, and if appropriate, those who have the overall responsibility for small group ministries in your church or organization.
- Remain a student of small groups in general, and of people in specific.
- Don't shy away from seeking help when you need it.
- Pace yourself.
- Find someone you can train to become a small group leader. And do it.
- Buy yourself an ice cream cone or some other small reward for having finished reading this book.

SHALOM

MORE SMALL GROUP HELPS FROM NEAL MCBRIDE.

How to Have Great Small-Group Meetings

Do your small-group meetings tend to wander off track?
Do you often feel unprepared? Here are the tools you need to
plan and lead small-group meetings that are efficient and effective.

How to Have Great Small-Group Meetings
$8

Real Small Groups Don't Just Happen

Think all it takes to make a small group is to gather people?
Think again. Real small groups don't just happen—they take work.
This book examines the elements necessary to create deeper
relationships and a functioning, healthy small-group community.

Real Small Groups Don't Just Happen
$9

How to Build a Small-Groups Ministry

This hands-on workbook gives you the twelve steps you need to
develop and administer an effective small-groups ministry. Includes
worksheets for creating a specialized ministry for your church.

How to Build a Small-Group Ministry
$20

Get your copies today at your local bookstore,
through our website, or by calling (800) 366-7788.
Ask for offer **#6001** or a FREE catalog of NavPress resources.

NAVPRESS
BRINGING TRUTH TO LIFE
www.navpress.com